Franciscan Spirituality

❧ *Franciscan Spirituality*
FOLLOWING ST FRANCIS TODAY

Brother Ramon SSF

Illustrations by Molly Dowell

First published in Great Britain 1994
Society for Promoting Christian Knowledge
Holy Trinity Church
Marylebone Road
London NW1 4DU

British Library Cataloguing-in-Publication Data
A catalogue record for this book is available from the British Library

ISBN 0-281-04721-9

Typeset by Action Typesetting Limited, Gloucester
Printed in Great Britain by
The Cromwell Press, Melksham, Wiltshire

Dedicated to
Members of the Third Order of
The Society of St Francis

Contents ✸

ABBREVIATIONS

1 Cel	Celano's *First Life of St Francis*
2 Cel	Celano's *Second Life of St Francis*
3S	*Legend of the Three Companions*
FB	*The Francis Book*, ed. Roy M. Gasnick OFM (London: Collier Macmillan, 1980)
Fior	*Fioretti* or *Little Flowers of St Francis*
LM	Major Life of St Francis by St Bonaventure
Lm	Minor Life of St Francis by St Bonaventure
Omn	*Omnibus of the Sources for the Life of St Francis*, ed. Marion A. Habig (Chicago: Franciscan Herald Press, 1973)
Sp	*Speculum Perfectionis* or *Mirror of Perfection*

Biblical quotations are from The New Revised Standard Version (NRSV).

Introduction: 🐦

A Distinctive Franciscan Flavour

When I was Guardian of our monastery in Worcester, one of my tasks was the making of the bread. I enjoyed that job, and the bread never failed to rise. But one day I forgot the salt! The friars noticed. The guests who were used to the taste of our bread noticed. I noticed and winced. All the joy, the flavour, the distinctive 'something' that made our Franciscan bread so edible and attractive, was lost. The result was ten insipid loaves that had to be eaten because we couldn't waste them — but this made the next batch all the more appreciated.

Describing and commending a participation in Franciscan spirituality is like the making and eating of wholesome monastery bread — 'Taste and see that the Lord is good.'

My aim in the following chapters is not to enter Franciscan spirituality in contemporary competitive stakes or to lay out a comparison-and-contrast table which commends the Franciscan approach before all others. This would result in a spiritual rat race or power game that is as far from the spirit of Francis and of Jesus as it is possible to go. After all, there have been some thoroughly bad Franciscans, and some of the holiest saints never heard of St Francis of Assisi.

The aim of this book is rather to bear joyful witness to an understanding of the gospel of Christ from a Franciscan perspective. By 'Franciscan spirituality' is meant a way of believing, of experiencing, of living and sharing in the wonder of creation and in the fullness of the gospel. It is a way in which the salt is present and active, giving a distinctive taste and sustaining power, and preserving life from insipidness and corruption.

Everything about such a spirituality is centred in Christ, rooted in creation and redemption, illustrated in the life of Francis himself, and in those in all three Franciscan Orders who seek to live in that tradition. But it is also inclusive, and open to everyone — not only every human being, but also every creature, and creation itself.

Theology is therefore closely interwoven with experience, sorrow with joy, humour with suffering, allowing the light of hope to shine in the darkest places of our humanity.

Franciscan spirituality is especially relevant to our own day. Not only does it ground us in the biblical faith from which the Franciscan experience springs, but it roots us into the very stuff of creation, with its immediate awareness of earth, sea, and sky.

Our environment is increasingly polluted by modern culture, industry, commerce, and warfare. Our natural resources are being depleted by the hour, and we are poisoning and infecting our fellow human beings and other creatures.

In such a world the Franciscan love of nature, reverence for life, and openness to our fellows leads to joy and peace, with a down-to-earth and practical desire to correct our mistakes and reverse our wrong practices.

In our own day, when political ideologies are collapsing, when religion is being exploited as an argument for exclusivism and violence, and when the poorer nations are calling for equality and justice, then the life and teaching of St Francis is a beacon in the darkness. In him the light of Christ shines most clearly, and the love of Christ continues to manifest itself.

EVOLVING SPIRITUALITIES

Over the last two decades there has been a boom in the exploration of particular spiritualities within and outside the Christian tradition.[1] Any issue of *Vision*, the organ of The Society for the Promotion of Retreats, will not only give the names and addresses of monastic/retreat houses throughout Britain, but also advertise retreats spanning a wide spectrum of spiritual approaches to suit everyone's tastes. They range from the Myers–Briggs' pattern of psychological types and Sufi Enneagram projects, to the traditional retreats according to the Benedictine, Ignatian, Carmelite, Dominican, or other perspectives.

All these are of value, and all have their appeal and followers. There is no doubt of the worth of the immensely popular Ignatian retreats undertaken by Christians of all traditions, and of the less well known but extremely valuable Benedictine retreats involving guided manual work, study, and prayer. The Carmelite tradition, with its emphasis on cell spirituality and the teachings of St John of the Cross and St Teresa of Avila, has been the backbone of many Christians' devotional lives for centuries.

These are all Christian spiritualities, with their different appeal and emphases, and they do not cancel each other out. But there are as many differing people as there are emphases, and though St Dominic was very keen to throw in his lot with St Francis, creating one Order, yet Francis knew that Dominic's way was not his way, and that the life in which Dominic would grow and thrive would simply choke him. Conversely, Dominic would have become exasperated with the spontaneity and uninhibited emotional freedom of Francis, which would have seemed to him like lack of planning, order, and control.

So in presenting this book on Franciscan spirituality, I am responding to a call from our Anglican Third Order, to put into a form of words something that will inform and inspire any Christian who is looking for a way to live out the gospel of Christ, whether they identify themselves with the way of Francis of Assisi or not.

It imparts a Franciscan perspective, a way of looking at the gospel, the Church, the world, and ourselves. This perspective is one that has enthused and inspired me as an individual on a difficult, lonely path, which is at the same time joyful, exciting, and fulfilling. It is also a perspective that has enthused and inspired me as a member of a Franciscan community, a Christian Church, and an evolving humanity. These groupings need all the discipline and spontaneity, the joy and sorrow, the justice, peace, and freedom from competitive inequalities that such a Franciscan perspective can impart.

A BROTHER AND SISTER TO ALL

I conclude this Introduction with two stories. Franciscans began as mendicant (begging) friars, and one of the ways in which this is still possible is by hitching a lift on an evangelistic or ministry trek. One day a lorry stopped on the A303 in the West Country in response to my 'thumbs up' sign. It is comparatively easy to get a lift in a Franciscan habit! As we sped along the driver asked: 'If you could tell me in one sentence what you stood for, what would you say?'

'Oh, that's not an easy question,' I replied, 'because I would want to say something about Jesus in my life. But if I could communicate my attitude in one sentence, I would say that I seek to be open to every other human being as my brother and sister.'

'Gosh, that's mind-blowing,' he responded. 'If everyone was like that, the world would change.' 'Hold on!' I grinned. 'I didn't say I actually *live* like that, but I want to.' So began a warm and friendly exchange.

My second story comes from the life of Martin Buber, the Jewish Hasidic philosopher. One day Buber was lecturing in New York, and took a taxi to a bookstore. During the journey, the young taxi driver looked at this old, bearded man and said: 'Father, I've been reading about a fellow who lived hundreds of years ago, gave away all his money and property, and went about in poverty following Jesus literally. Do you know anything about him?'

'Ah yes,' answered Buber, 'you are talking about St Francis of Assisi. I know quite a few stories about him.' Soon the two of them were lost in the wonder and joy of Francis and the thirteenth century, in the middle of the New York traffic.

All too soon they arrived at the destination. They bade one another a smiling farewell, and Buber went into the bookstore. Soon he discovered that he had lost his spectacles, but just then, the door opened and the young 'cabbie' entered, looked around, and came up to Buber.

He put his head on Buber's shoulder, saying, 'Father, I found yours "specs" in my cab.' 'Thank you my son,' said Buber, and put his arm around him.

If Franciscan spirituality is to be made real and valid in our contemporary world, it has to be believed and lived with such immediacy and relevance as this — a Jewish philosopher and a New York cab driver!

If I follow in the Franciscan path, it is a following of Jesus in a distinctive way, in which the heights and depths of human experience are lived out and shared. It is living joyfully, sharing compassionately, and dying well.

And that is only the beginning!

Ramon SSF
The Society of St Francis

1 ✺ *Looking for Francis of Assisi*

Nikos Kazantzakis pictures Francis sitting in the wintry sun at the Portiuncula Church of St Mary and the Angels. A young man comes running up to him, breathless, and stands before him:

'Where is Francis, Bernadone's son?' he asked, his tongue hanging out of his mouth. 'Where can I find the new saint so that I may fall at his feet? For months now I have been roaming the streets looking for him. For the love of Christ, my brother, tell me where he is.'

'Where is Francis, Bernadone's son?' replied Francis, shaking his head. 'Where is Francis, Bernadone's son? What is this Francis? Who is he? I am looking for him also, my brother. I have been looking for him now for years. Give me your hand let us go find him.'[1]

Francis was born in Assisi in Umbrian Italy in 1182. His father was Pietro di Bernadone, a wealthy fabric merchant, and his mother, Pica, was probably French. He was baptized John by his mother when Pietro was in France, and on his return his father called him Francis, the name that stuck.

Francis was likeable, sensitive, fun-loving, and gregarious. As the years went by, his love of poetry, love songs, and the troubadour romantic tradition brought to light hidden passion and ambition.

He learned some French from his father's journeyings, and perhaps, from his mother. Childhood lessons were taken at St Giorgio's church school, and he listened to many stories of medieval chivalry and knightly glory and courage in the service of a liege lord.

His military dreams were soon shattered. He was taken prisoner in a battle between Assisi and Perugia, and spent a year in a Perugian prison, after which he suffered prolonged fever.

In 1204, he set out to fight in a papal army in Apulia. But twenty-five miles out of Assisi, Francis had a mystical experience which told him to return to Assisi. This was the beginning of his conversion, for he then received a startling vision of the crucified Jesus and began to seek God in solitude and prayer.

For months he prayed through the light and darkness of dawning faith, sharing his anguish and yearning with a trusted friend whom some have thought to be Elias Bombarone, who, in the eyes of the later 'Spiritual' friars, became the villain of the piece.

Francis became even freer with his father's money, distributing it among the poor. He filched and sold some bolts of Pietro's best cloth in the market at Foligno, the proceeds of which were refused by the poor parish priest of San Damiano's church, a mile outside Assisi.

He then made a pilgrimage to Rome, and exchanged his clothes with a pauper outside St Peter's, and begged all day in lousy rags — an experience of identification!

Hating and fearing loathsome leprosy, he found himself embracing a leper near Assisi, and this completely changed his attitude. Soon afterwards, praying with fervour and longing in the tumbledown San Damiano church, the Christ of the crucifix said to him: 'Francis, go and repair my Church which, as you see, is falling into ruins.'

Before he had a chance to begin such a work literally, his father, enraged by the sale of his expensive fabrics at Foligno, summoned Francis before Bishop Guido's court in Assisi. Here, in 1206, occurred the dramatic act of stripping himself naked as a mark of complete renunciation of his family and the world, for God. So began twenty years of loving service to God, and the literal following of Christ in poverty.

During the next two years, in hermit dress he repaired three small churches near Assisi – San Damiano, San Pietro, and St Mary of the Angels – the Portiuncula.

It was there, on the Feast of St Matthias in 1209, that God spoke to him in the reading of the Gospel at mass from St Matthew 10.7–10, outlining the pattern of the life which Francis yearned for. His literal obedience to Scripture caused him to throw away his staff, take off his sandals, and exchange his leather belt for a rope. The Order of Friars Minor had begun.

Within weeks, three companions joined him. They were Bernard of Quintivalle, Peter Catanii, and Giles of Assisi. The number soon reached twelve, and Francis composed a Rule of gospel texts. He boldly travelled to Rome with his eleven companions to get it approved by Pope Innocent III. His audacity was rewarded with a verbal approval. It was probably on this occasion that he was ordained deacon. For humility's sake, he never sought the priesthood.

The twelve friars were levered out of a shed at Rivo Torto by a pushy donkeyman, and were given the Portiuncula by the Mount Subasio Benedictines. Their numbers increased, and, on Palm Sunday night 1212, Francis received into the Order the eighteen-year-old Clare Offreduccio, who eventually became Abbess of the Second Order of Poor Clares.

In 1212, and again in 1213, Francis failed to reach the Muslim lands in the hope of preaching and martyrdom. In 1215, at the Lateran Council in Rome, he began a lifelong friendship with St Dominic. In 1217, at the General Chapter, he volunteered to go to France, but Cardinal Hugolino (later Pope Gregory IX) persuaded him to remain in Italy. The opportunity to join the Crusaders came in 1219, and, leaving two vicars to govern the Order, he went to

Damietta in Egypt and preached to the Sultan Malek-el-Kamel.

His trials began in 1220, when he returned to Italy, suffering from malaria and glaucoma, and found that the process of deterioration and backsliding had come into the open under the two vicars. Soon he obtained from Pope Honorius III the appointment of Cardinal Hugolino as the Order's Protector, and he resigned as Minister, naming Peter Catanii in his place. Peter died the next year, 1221, and Brother Elias succeeded him.

Francis wrote the Gospel Rule of 1221, but because of its length, eloquence, and scriptural demands, he had to revise and rewrite it twice before it was approved as the *Regula Bullata* in 1223.

Francis' understanding of his Order of Poor Friars was not based on Benedictine, Augustinian, or any other monastic rule. It embraced the three vows of poverty, chastity, and obedience, but this was an expression of the life of Christ in the gospel. He saw this as a mendicant, itinerant life, divided between prayer and preaching, and supported by manual work and begging. The strict poverty was personal and communal. All this flowed towards, and was an expression of, an ever-deepening union with God in Christ, and the inspiration of the Holy Spirit pervaded the whole enterprise. Yet, unlike so many sects and reformers, Francis maintained and demanded loyalty to the Catholic Church and reverence for its priests.

As the Order grew, and especially under the two vicars and Brother Elias, there were various compromises and a relaxation of gospel principles. This was because of a failure to grasp the central Christ-mysticism and literal following of the poor Jesus. In their place, recourse was had to traditional monastic conventual life, an intellectual apostolate, and a laxer life-style.

Under the influence of Cardinal Hugolino, Francis was persuaded towards some modification and adaptation because of the increase in numbers and the educational and missionary demands of the Church. This was against Francis' vision and intuition, and he maintained to the end the strict adherence to poverty and gospel simplicity in his personal life, as an example to the friars. This was his 'dark night', and he only emerged from it when he received a revelation and inward assurance that Christ would always remain the first Head of the Order, so that those friars who wished to follow Christ in the light of Francis would be enabled to do so. It was with Cardinal Hugolino's help that Francis instituted the Third Order around 1221.

In 1223, Francis erected the Bethlehem crib at Greccio with the mystical joy of holding the Christ-child in his arms. This prepared him for the seal of mystical union with Christ which he experienced on Mount La Verna in 1224 — the imprinting of the five wounds of the stigmata on his body, in answer to his prayer that he might enter into the suffering and love of Christ's passion.

He lived for two more years, with much suffering of body and spirit, but with interior joy and saintly influence. During this period of weakness he composed his *Canticle of Brother Sun* at San Damiano, in his blindness, and he produced his *Testament*, which preserves his gospel vision of simplicity.

During his last illness he was moved to his beloved Portiuncula, where he was laid naked on the ground, following the example of the naked Christ on the cross — the clear expression of *Il Poverello*, the Little Poor Man, who said: 'I have done my duty; may Christ teach you yours.'

He died peacefully on 3 October 1226, and just two years later was canonized by his friend and admirer Pope Gregory IX.

O Lord Jesus Christ:
You raised up Francis to renew in your Church the life
of simplicity and evangelical poverty,
and imprinted on his flesh the marks of your wounds;
Pour out your Spirit on us, that following you in the
nakedness of the cross, and bearing your wounds in
our hearts,
we may at length attain to your perfect likeness,
who with the Father and the Holy Spirit, live and
reign, one God, now and for ever. Amen.[2]

2 ❧ *Galilee, Umbria, and Where I Am*

Christians of different traditions often look back with a certain yearning and wistfulness to an era in which their particular understanding of the faith was affirmed with clarity and truth. The life and teaching of Jesus, consummated in his death and resurrection, were told out in the Palestine of the first century, and much of it around the region of the Lake of Galilee. And even as adults it is possible for us to sing that children's hymn:

> I think when I read that sweet story of old,
> When Jesus was here among men,

How he called little children as lambs to his fold,
  I should like to have been with him then.
I wish that his hands had been placed on my head,
  That his arms had been thrown around me,
And that I might have seen his kind look when he said,
  'Let the little ones come unto Me.'

Some contemporary Christians look back to an age in which the gospel was free of the trammels of establishment, in the days of courage, persecution, and purity before the 'conversion' of the Emperor Constantine.

There is at present a continuing revival of interest in the era immediately following that edict of imperial favour. It charts the lives and sayings of the Desert Fathers (and Mothers) of Palestine, Egypt, Arabia, and Persia from the fourth century, and, following hard upon that, the Celtic monastic tradition of Britain.

Orthodox Christians may look back to Byzantine greatness, while Roman Catholics yearn for the unity which the Church enjoyed before the separation of East and West in the eleventh century and the Reformation of the sixteenth.

The Reformation itself provides a pattern for many Protestant Christians, while there has always been a desire and attempt to reach back to the simplicity and harmony of the New Testament Church.

An examination of the Acts and Epistles portrays also confusion and disharmony, but the desire for early purity, joy, and apostolic pattern has never ceased to stimulate both unity and schism.

FRANCIS, 'THE ONLY PERFECT CHRISTIAN'[1]

Part of the greatness of Francis, with his roots in Umbria, the green heart of Italy, is his universal appeal. As Omer Englebert says in his preface to *Saint Francis of Assisi*:

It is not only Catholics who form the retinue of his admirers; Protestants, Pantheists, Rationalists and indifferents have their place. Even certain Buddhists feel themselves in relation with him, and when Gandhi makes the work of his hands, his love for the Untouchables and non-resistance to evil the base of his religious reform, one has to ask oneself whether he too has not borrowed from the Franciscan programme of Rivo Torto.[2]

11

In the Umbria of the thirteenth century, and spreading to other parts of Italy, Europe, and the wider world, Christ was not simply imitated by St Francis, but incarnated and manifested in such a way that the philosopher Renan was constrained to say that 'after Jesus he was the only perfect Christian'.

St Francis' words and deeds transported people back to Galilee; the celebration of the Christmas crib at Greccio recalled Bethlehem; the mysterious wounds of the stigmata on Mount La Verna told again the story of Mount Calvary.

To be in the company of Francis on the path of discipleship and service was to walk again the roads of Palestine in the company of Jesus and his disciples, to hear again the words of the gospel in their immediacy, to see again men and women forgiven, healed, given hope in their despair, and a pattern of meaning and service in a life of compassion and simplicity. That is why the prayer ascribed to Francis seems to sum up the attraction which is universal:

> Lord, make me an instrument of your peace.
> Where there is hatred, let me sow love;
> Where there is injury, pardon;
> Where there is doubt, faith;
> Where there is despair, hope;
> Where there is darkness, light;
> Where there is sadness, joy.
> O Divine Master, grant that I may not so much
>   seek to be consoled as to console,
> to be understood as to understand,
> to be loved as to love.
> For it is in giving that we receive,
> it is in pardoning that we are pardoned,
> and it is in dying that we are born to
>   eternal life. Amen.

NOT FRANCIS, BUT CHRIST

It would be the greatest of mistakes to be a follower of Francis and not of Christ. This would be impossible when confronted with the wholeness of Francis' life and teaching. But it has been a widespread error to make Francis the patron saint of nature and ecology, a lover of wild creatures and domesticated pets, a lover of earth, sea, and sky, and then to evade the centre, the primary thing, the gospel and the mystical imperative of surrender to Christ.

Francis was not a footloose and fancy-free hippie who set up a religious commune to get back to nature. Neither can you appeal to Francis in justification of the luxurious coddling and expensive feeding of some of our pets while most of the world cries out in hunger and deprivation.

I am not among those who despise animal services. I enjoy mingling with adults and children who bring their pets for blessing at a joyful Franciscan festival, but I always take the opportunity of affirming the centrality of Christ, which is to be true to the Franciscan pattern. Thomas of Celano says of Francis:

> 'He was always occupied with Jesus; Jesus he bore in his heart, Jesus in his mouth, Jesus in his ears, Jesus in his eyes, Jesus in his hands, Jesus in the rest of his members.'[3]

The whole meaning of discipline and asceticism in the life of Francis was the outcome of his love for Jesus. His simplicity and poverty was the bringing of his life into conformity with the way of Jesus. It was not asceticism for asceticism's sake, or poverty as an antidote to luxury and waste, or even as a rebuke to a worldly and luxurious Church or state, but a living out of the simplicity and discipline of a follower of Jesus.

If Francis wanted his friars and sisters to follow the way of his Rule, it was because the Rule embodied the gospel and was given him by God, and because he would say with St Paul: 'Be imitators of me, as I am of Christ.'[4]

WHERE I AM

The leading question that God asked the hidden Adam in the Garden of Eden at the cool of the day was: 'Where are you?' It was both a geographical and an existential question. God begins with us where we are, not where we are not!

It seemed to most professing Christians in Francis' day, especially among the hierarchy, that it was impossible to live the gospel as completely and as literally as Francis understood it. Palestine had little to do with Italy, and Galilee could not be planted again in Umbria. The whole Franciscan story, as far as Francis and his followers were concerned, showed that this is exactly what *could* be done, what *should* be done, and ultimately what *was* done.

The question which arises in a viable Franciscan spirituality for today is whether what happened in Palestine in the story of Jesus, and what was lived out in the story of Francis in Italy, is possible in this day and age, *where we are — where I am*. It has to be personal and it has to be corporate — but can it be at all?

As we start out on such an enquiring journey with Francis and his followers, let us take note of one important thing. The kind of spirituality which underlies any telling of the story of Francis is one which involves and calls into play all the positive faculties and emotions of which our humanity is capable.

It is a spirituality of wholeness that is *spiritual* in answering to the needs of the profoundest spiritual quest, and true to the biblical tradition.

It is *intellectual*, not in the sense that it aspires to great learning — Francis certainly teaches us to beware of that — but in that it is in the wisdom tradition of the great sages and intuitive thinkers. It therefore calls all the powers of the mind to an application of the gospel, producing a radical personal and economic revolution that would threaten any materialistic political stance.[5]

It is *emotional* in that it calls for a participation of all our feeling faculties. The life and preaching of the early Franciscans involved not only the lifting up of the voice, but of the heart, eyes, ears, hands, and feet. There was sighing and gesticulation, laughing and crying, singing and weeping, dancing and mourning. The common people, during market-place preaching, could taste the honey of the gospel or could even smell the good odour of holiness or the bad smell of the devil and the judgement to come. St Bonaventure, in a typical eulogy of Francis, wrote: 'Jesus Christ crucified reposed continually on the breast of Francis like a bouquet of myrrh, and the fire of love with which he burned made him desire to be entirely transformed into Jesus.'[6]

A spirituality which can call forth all human powers of mind and heart is one which must command attention in days when there is much subjectivity in religion. If a person's faith has no real relevance to the various levels at which life is lived, it becomes a ghetto religion. Mysticism without overt political implications and action is no better than a social gospel without a sense of transcendence and the miracle-working power of God in human life.

The transformation which the gospel brings about, according to Franciscan spirituality, is grounded in the conversion of the whole person and an elevation of all the faculties of body, mind, and spirit in making life more human and more divine. Human compassion goes hand in hand with mystical prayer, and the transformation of the human personality by the Holy Spirit must lead to the transfiguration of human life in its personal, social, and political aspects.

The corporate, communal, social, and political implications of all this will be spelled out as we progress, but our discipleship must be rooted in a personal confrontation with oneself and with God in penitence and faith. There must be no lessening of the personal when the individual joins with others in the spiritual and human tasks of compassion and service.

There is a typical glimpse of Franciscan spirituality in a poem of Jacopone da Todi that revels in the sensual yet spiritual assault of the divine Love upon his body and soul with implications that embrace the whole created order. Jacopone may well have composed this poem after his dark, dank, and miserable privation of five years in an underground dungeon in Palestrina:

> *O Love Divine, You besiege my heart:*
> *You are crazed with love for me, and cannot rest.*

My five senses are assaulted by You,
Hearing, sight, taste, touch and scent,
Love, You woo me and I cannot hide from You.

I gaze through my eyes and see Love all around
In radiance and colour, in earth, sea and sky,
Drowning in such beauty, You draw me to Yourself.

I open my ears to music,
Entranced by the woven mist of loveliness,
Creation's chanting of Your name.

I taste and savour Your sweetness,
You hunger and thirst for me,
And You are my medicine and food.

Your perfume breathes through all creation,
I am held and wounded by Your odour,
For all creatures give forth the fragrance of Your beauty.

If I stretch out my hands to touch,
You are sculptured in all fair forms,
You inflame me with desire for Your love.

I flee from You and yet I cannot escape,
You yearn to melt me in Your love,
Oh, to be possessed by Love's fiery embrace.

So lead me to Christ, my fair Love,
To share the wounds and griefs that He bore,
Patterned throughout creation.

This sensual and spiritual experience of grace and nature was not confined to Jacopone, but shared with his Franciscan sisters and brothers like Ramon Lull, James of Massa, John of La Verna, Angelo of Foligno, Margaret of Cortona — right down to the present generation of Franciscans throughout the world.

It is Francis' universal vision and experience that inspires the immediacy of the joy and sorrow of Christ in the present moment. The *Poverello* of Assisi is a universal saint by his wisdom and by his acts of seeming emotionalism and tomfoolery. But here also is a man who appeals to us by the transparent honesty of heart and sincerity of purpose that he reveals throughout his story. He is not afraid to laugh and cry, to kiss the outcast leper or exchange clothes with a filthy beggar. He can't help but sing because of the joy of forgiveness and divine love. He can't help but weep because his dear and suffering Saviour is neglected and abused by indifference and hostility.[7]

We shall find, as we follow his steps and the steps of his own followers, that if our minds and hearts are open to God, we too shall be drawn into the fellowship of Francis that encircles the world, and shall discover a spirituality which interprets Christ's gospel for our lives and our day.

Lord Jesus Christ:
You walked the roads of Umbria in the days of Francis our
 father as you walked the roads of Galilee in the days of
 your earthly ministry;
Walk with us in the paths of our daily lives, and let your
 love be incarnate again in the hearts of all people;
To the praise of your holy name. Amen.

3 *Troubadour Romanticism*

BUILDING A WALL AROUND ASSISI

In 1198, when Francis was sixteen years old, Innocent III became pope. One of his first acts was to eject Conrad of Lutzen from the

Rocca castle of Assisi. Conrad met Pope Innocent at Narni and signed the surrender.

As soon as the people of Assisi heard the news, they became wild with joy, razed the Rocca to the ground, and used much of the stone to build a wall around their city. The news, the celebrations, and the building excited young and old, and doubtless Francis was caught up in it; and, it may have been here that he learned the craft of building which would be converted to good in repairing churches within a decade.

It was not military might or the political implications that interested the young Francis in the events which led to the skirmish between Perugia and Assisi in 1202 when he was twenty years old. There was a romantic feeling of independence and pride of place in the life of Assisi, together with the growing power of the Commune, and Francis was the son of one of the richest merchants. The taking of the stone from the abandoned castle and the building of a protecting ring around Assisi was a participation in a romantic movement within the national and religious ferment of disputation between pope and emperor, and was of a piece in Francis' mind with some of the chivalrous elements of the troubadour tradition which had been woven into his imagination since childhood.

TROUBADOURS AND JONGLEURS

The troubadours were composers of poems and love songs. They roamed the towns of north and mid-Italy at that time, singing of courtly love and knightly exploits in the Provençal tongue. The jongleurs did not invent or compose, but sang the songs of the troubadours, and were called upon to supply entertainment at functions in the courts and castles, and were also found at market squares and busy crossroads. They sang of Charlemagne, Arthur, Guinevere and Merlin, of the Holy Grail, of Tristram, and of Roland.

Francis would have been especially fascinated by such groups because he may well have travelled with his father in search of fine fabrics in France, picking up some French and Provençal along the way. All this may have built upon the foundation of stories and songs from his mother, Pica, if the tradition which speaks of her Provençal background is true.[1]

Songs of courtly love and knightly exploits filled the air with a

code of courtesy and chivalry, especially towards women. Francis'
romance with Lady Poverty may have had its beginnings here, for
the troubadour lady remained the inaccessible ideal of a knight in
romantic rapture — and the cost was voluntary chastity. Marriage
would have spoiled such idealized love that found fulfilment in
death. A song from that tradition makes it plain:

> But I have so much pleasure in wishing it so
> That I suffer agreeably,
> And so much joy in my pain
> That I am sick with delight.[2]

This was the mysterious beloved referred to by Francis when he
was found wandering trancelike after being lost during one of the
night revels of the young bloods of Assisi.[3] Englebert, quoting Don
Quixote, wrote: 'there is never a knight without a Lady, any more
than there are trees without leaves or sky without stars'. Then he
comments: 'But the love they sang was that which sacrifice and
fidelity purified, for the heroes whose exploits they magnified were
always *Chevaliers sans peur et sans reproche.*'

> In the life of St Francis, at every step we shall think of the
> *Chansons de Geste* of the troubadours and of the jongleurs too.
> Like Rinaud de Montauban, the cousin of Roland, we shall see
> him build churches to expiate his past faults; like King Arthur,
> he gathers his companions about the Round Table in a chapel
> at Pentecost; he will compose verses and music, he will sing the
> divine praises while pretending to accompany himself on a viol,
> and we shall hear him without ceasing use the vocabulary of the
> *poesies courtoises* to express his soul and draw men after him.[4]

Francis called his friars 'my true knights of the Round Table',
and as troubadours of Christ wanted them to go singing in joy
and tears around the world. 'Since we are the jongleurs of God,'
he said, 'and deserve some reward for our songs, what we ask of
you is that you live henceforth as good Christians.'[5]

FRANCIS AS TROUBADOUR

In the year 1213, Francis and Leo were evangelizing around
Montefeltre when they arrived at the fortress built on a spur
of the Apennines. One of the Counts of Montefeltro was being
knighted on that day, and crowds filled the square accompanied

by the sound of minstrels from the castle court. As Francis went with Leo in the crowd, he felt the power of the Holy Spirit upon him.

One of the troubadour minstrels had just sung a song of love and suffering for the sake of the beloved, including the words:

> Tanto e il bene ch'aspetto
> Ch'ogni pena m'e diletto ...

Flags and banners were waving as the music died down and the people applauded. Suddenly Francis climbed on to a low wall, and taking up the same words, he began:

> So great is the happiness I look for
> that every pain is a pleasure ...

and he preached with great fervour on the sufferings of the apostles, martyrs, confessors, and knights of Christ who endured much pain for the love of their liege-man and Saviour, Jesus. Knights, nobles, and ladies were enthused, among whom was the young Count of Chiusi, Orlando. As a result of Francis' inspired preaching, Orlando gave his life to Christ, and joyfully gifted his mountain in Tuscany to Francis. This was Mount La Verna, which became, as the later friars described it, *molto divota, e molto atta a contemplare,* 'a very devout and apt place for contemplation'.[6]

This was eleven years before the stigmata took place on that holy mountain, but already the way was being prepared – that most profound contemplative experience growing out of Francis' troubadour ministry.

SONGS OF JOY AND SORROW

Franciscan spirituality carries no monopoly on the heights and depths of Christian experience. But it is a spirituality of experience rather than scholastic dogmatism. The typical Franciscan is a man or woman in love, and people in love feel and do extraordinary things.[7] They are intoxicated with the love of God, sometimes shouting their exuberance from the highest hill, and at other times sharing the sorrow of Calvary, weeping with the despised and rejected Jesus.

There may also be dramatic swings of mood as the lover experiences the penetrating touch of the Holy Spirit in the ecstasy of adoration, and then suddenly realizes the cost of redemption – the

shedding of the precious blood of Christ. This is continually demonstrated in the life of Francis, and it is stated succinctly in the
Mirror of Perfection:

> Intoxicated by love and compassion for Christ, blessed Francis
> sometimes used to act in ways like these. For the sweetest of
> spiritual melodies would often well up within him and found
> expression in French melodies, and then murmurs of God's
> voice, heard by him alone, would joyfully pour forth in the
> French tongue.
>
> Sometimes he would pick up a stick from the ground, and
> laying it on his left arm, he would draw another stick across it
> with his right hand like a bow, as though he were playing a viol
> or some other instrument; and he would imitate the movements
> of a musician and sing in French of our Lord Jesus Christ.
>
> But all this jollity would end in tears, and his joy would melt
> away in compassion for the sufferings of Christ. And at such
> times he would break into constant sighs, and in his grief would
> forget what he was holding in his hands, and be caught up in
> spirit into heaven.[8]

It is expected that Franciscans should be full of joy – even among
those who do not share their faith. A while ago, travelling from
Worcester to Exeter on the M5, I hitched a lift and was picked
up by a burly, tough, and humorous lorry driver. We pulled in
at a motorway café for some coffee, and soon two coachloads of
schoolchildren trundled in.

One of the mischievous lads of about ten years old looked over
at my brown habit and grinned: 'Are you Friar Tuck?' he enquired.
'No,' I replied, 'but I belong to the same family.' Then he looked
at the macho lorry driver. 'Who's he?' he asked, 'Maid Marion?'
The driver laughed with all the children and shook his fist at the
boy, and one of the teachers intervened: 'That's enough, Roberts,'
and there was a murmuring of chuckling good humour about the
episode.

It was expected that I would be joyful, that I would engage in
repartee, and that I would give as good as I got – that's what a
friar is for! People in the world expect it. But if I had been discovered weeping at the side of the road, as Francis often was,
entering more deeply into the sorrow of Christ in his passion, or
for the world's pain, then the same people would be perplexed.

Francis would censure a friar who went about with a gloomy

face when he should have been radiating the joy of creation and salvation. Such a brother or sister would not only detract from the joy of God in the world, but could become a depressing and negative influence in the community. He would say:

> Why are you making an outward display of grief and sorrow for your sin? This sorrow is between God and yourself alone. So pray Him in His mercy to pardon you and restore to your soul the joy of His salvation, of which the guilt of your sin has deprived it. Always do your best to be cheerful when you are with me and the other brethren; it is not right for a servant of God to show a sad and gloomy face to his brother or to anyone else.[9]

But on the other hand he would not allow shallow levity or empty laughter and gossip, for these are not evidences of spiritual joy, but of a superficial life-style and deterioration in community life. All the world loves a lover, and although there may be many experiences of tears and sorrows (as there must be in any genuine life of love), there is a joyful sharing and openness to others on the way of salvation, and a troubadour desire to sing and proclaim the beloved.

PARADOX, NOT CONTRADICTION

There is a sense in which the troubadour lover is a sign of contradiction in a world dominated by self-love and egocentricity. In Christian and Franciscan terms, the gospel itself contradicts materialism and the political power structures which are alien to justice and peace. But there is no internal contradiction in the lover or the Franciscan Christian. The poles of joy and sorrow, of singing and weeping, of restless yearning and joyful discovery, are part of the wholeness of such a life. Mystical experience of God causes ordinary people to behave in extraordinary ways.

Richard Rolle, the fourteenth-century Yorkshire hermit and mystic, distinguished three phases of mystical fervour — *calor* (heat), *canor* (melody), and *dulcor* (sweetness), and his description could easily be taken as Franciscan experience.

In his *Fire of Love*, he speaks of sitting in chapel in meditation when he felt within him a 'merry and unknown heat [*calor*]'. He is quite adamant that this is not simply a subjective experience, but is given by God. After about a year there was added 'an incoming and receiving of a heavenly and spiritual sound [*canor*]'. This spiritual melody, he says, comes to one surrendered to God. His response was to burst out in psalms and singing, and then he became enamoured of 'a feeling of great inward sweetness [*dulcor*]'.

This is the kind of experiential religion which is at the heart of Franciscan spirituality. The Franciscan troubadour *par excellence*, Jacopone da Todi, used a technical term, *Jubilus*, to denote the evangelical fervour that lays hold of the believer who is in love with God:

> O Jubilus of the heart, thou makest us sing of love. When the Jubilus is scalding hot, it makes a man sing, and his tongue stammers, and does not know what it says. He cannot hide the sweetness within him, it is so great ... When the Jubilus has seized on the enamoured heart, folk have it in derision.[10]

This is the *Jubilus* which makes the believer sing for joy and weep for pain, enslaving the heart and dazzling the mind. The world cannot understand it, and onlookers mock the behaviour of one caught up in such a movement of love.

The paradox is made explicit in Jacopone's poem on 'The Contemplation of the Cross'. He puts it into the form of a dialogue between two friars, to express the two parts of himself, alternately *warmed* and *burned* by the fire of love.

In Francis' experience, the two poles are expressed in the evangelical moment of forgiveness and vocation which he felt at the crucifix at San Damiano at the beginning of his pilgrimage, and then by the searing stigmata to which he was exposed towards the end of his life on Mount La Verna.

The model of two friars which Jacopone uses spells out the paradox of the two experiences which belong together in the integrated and sanctified friar or sister. This is inexplicable to the mere dogmatician, but is well known in the profound wisdom of the mystical tradition. There is even perplexity and confusion in the mind of the experiencing friar (as Jacopone well knew). God deals gently with the soul within the warm glow of his merciful forgiveness, but painfully in the searing flame of the divine Love:

> 1 I flee the Cross that does my heart devour,
>   I cannot bear its ardour and its power.
>
>   I cannot bear this great and dreadful heat;
>   Far from the Cross, from Love, on flying feet
>   I haste away; my heart at every beat
>   Consumes me with that burning memory.

2 Brother, why do you flee from this delight?
   This is the joy I yearn for, day and night.
   Brother, this is but weakness in my sight,
      To flee from joy and peace so cravenly.

1 Brother, I flee, for I am wounded sore,
   My heart is pierced and sundered to the core;
   You have not felt the anguish that I bore,
      Else you would speak in other words to me.

2 Brother, I find the Cross all garlanded,
   And with its blossoms do I wreathe my head;
   It wounds me not — no, I am comforted;
      The Cross is all delight and joy to me.

1 I find it full of arrows sharp, that dart
   Forth from its side: they reach, they pierce my heart!
   The Archer aims His shafts that tear and smart;
      And through my armour He has wounded me.

2 I once was blind, but now I see the light;
   Gazing upon the Cross I found my sight.
   Beneath the Cross my soul is glad and bright;
      Far from the Cross I am in misery.

1 Not so with me: this Light has made me blind!
   So fierce the lustre that around me shined,
   My heart is giddy and confused my mind,
      My eyes are dazzled that I cannot see.

2 Now can I speak, I that was once so dumb;
   'Tis from the Cross that all my powers come;
   Yes, by that Cross, of Thought and Love the Sum,
      Now I can preach to men full potently.

1 The Cross has made me dumb, who once spoke well;
   In such a deep abyss my heart does dwell,
   I cannot speak, and nothing can I tell;
      And none can understand or talk with me.

2 Lo, I was dead, and now new life is mine,
   Life that was given to me by the Cross divine:
   Yes, parted from the Cross, in death I pine,
      Its presence gives me all vitality.

1 I am not dead, but dying day by day;
Would God that I were dead and passed away!
Eternally I struggle, gasp and pray —
    And nothing I can do can set me free.

  2 Brother, the Cross to me is all delight;
    Beneath it dwells no torment or affright:
    Perhaps you have not felt that Union's might,
        Nor that Embrace that clasps so tenderly.

1 Ah, you are warmed; but I am in the Fire:
Yours the delight, but mine the flaming Pyre;
I cannot breathe within this furnace dire,
    Or bear the flame of Love's intensity.

  2 Brother, your words I cannot understand:
    Why do you flee from gentle Love's demand?
    Tell me your state, and let me take your hand,
        And let me listen to this mystery.

1 Brother, you breathe the perfume of the Wine;
But I have drunk It, and no strength of mine
Can bear the onslaught of such Love divine,
    That Lover ceases not to rapture me.[11]

TEMPERAMENT OF THE LOVER

Although Francis had no taste for book learning, and was always suspicious of scholarship within the Order, he loved the stories of the Round Table and of the other chivalrous romances we have referred to. Knightly adventures in the cause of the Church, Crusades, liege men, or beloved lady were in the very atmosphere of twelfth-century Italy. His was the temperament of the lover, and in the relationship of love was resolved the tensions of spontaneity and discipline, joy and sorrow, solitude and sharing, seeking and finding. His spiritual journey was a pilgrimage of love.

Father Cuthbert places Francis in this context, listening to the troubadour voices as they passed their fingers deftly and thrillingly over the varied strings of human emotion. Their songs of courage, endurance, and glory were always passionate, and even when they were sung to a human note they always seemed to carry the consistency of faith. Personal devotion and unselfish endurance for the sake of the cause or the beloved inspired their themes. So the language of Provence invaded the courts of the Italian nobles, sending a haunting voice into the air 'which set the heart of youth astir and was as a fresh breeze amidst the pessimism which had so long depressed the vitality of the peninsula'.[12]

You are my Beloved, Lord, and I love you;
It is my greatest sadness that I weep in your absence,
  and my greatest joy that I rejoice in your presence;
In days of darkness sustain the warmth of love and hope,
  and when you visit me in mercy, may my life shine with
  the radiance of your glory;
For you are my Beloved, and I am your lover. Amen.

4 ❧ *Suffering and Disillusion*

A REALISTIC SPIRITUALITY

There is a widespread image of Francis as a romantic and dreamy nature-mystic who neither saw nature 'red in tooth and claw' nor faced up to the violence and sinfulness of unaided and fallen humanity. The real Francis stands in stark contrast to such a cardboard image, facing resolutely all the ills to which creatures are heir in their finitude and mortality, and the inhumanity between human beings which reduces so many of them to suffering victims in a world of injustice and cruelty.

In 1202, when he was twenty years old, Francis took part in the bloody confrontation between Perugia and Assisi in the battle of Ponte San Giovanni on the Tiber. He was confronted there with the violence of war of which a Perugian poet wrote:

Fallen are the lords of Assisi, and their limbs are all mangled,
Torn apart and defaced, so their own cannot know them;
There is no head where the foot is, their entrails are scattered.
The eye no longer looks from the socket, its one-time window.[1]

Francis was taken prisoner by the Perugians, and because of his father's merchant status he found himself with the knights who, as Celano says, 'were consumed with sorrow, bemoaning miserably their imprisonment'.

But Francis laughed at his chains and rejoiced in the Lord, so that his companions thought him mad. His response to their attitude was prophetic: 'Why do you think I rejoice?' he asked. 'I will yet be venerated throughout the whole world.' And he turned his care and attention to a proud and unbearable knight who had been shunned by the rest, and was the means of reconciliation, so great was his charismatic charm and kindness.[2]

This mood did not last. He needed to learn the lesson of sickness and psychological depression. Perhaps the legacy of the violence and imprisonment only showed itself after his release. Anyway, soon after returning home he became ill of a fever. He had never enjoyed good health, and some have thought that his imprisonment, hidden from the light and beauty of the world, and exposed to infection, brought on tuberculosis.

After a few weeks in bed, he struggled out on sticks, and beneath the shadow of Mount Subasio he looked over the spring beauty of the Umbrian plain stretched before him. This was what he had yearned for in prison and through his weeks of fever. But now no sense of delight, joy, or hope filled him. Instead there was dryness, emptiness, and heaviness of heart.

He was astonished at this change, but he had to learn the bitter lesson that unless the springtime of love and forgiveness bursts to life in the heart, the world will be empty of meaning or joy. As Sabatier comments, he felt a discouragement a thousandfold more painful than any physical ill: 'The miserable emptiness of his life suddenly appeared before him; he was terrified at his solitude, the solitude of a great soul in which there is no altar.'[3]

THE EXPERIENCE DEEPENS

There was another attempt at self-fulfilment before his conversion. As soon as he was well enough, he turned his thoughts to chivalry and knightly glory again. Francis learned that Count Gentile of Assisi was preparing to depart for Apulia to join the armies of Walter de Brienne on behalf of the Church against the empire. This was a chance, perhaps, to become a knight.

His mind was full of dreams of military glory and chivalry as he set out towards Spoleto, where they rested. But in the night, by dream or vision, God spoke clearly to Francis and shattered his hope of knightly ambition.

After questioning him as to his destination and goal, another question came, asking who could do better for him, the servant or the lord. 'The lord,' replied Francis. 'Why then,' said the mysterious voice, 'are you seeking the servant in place of the Lord?' And Francis asked: 'Lord, what do you want me to do?' and the Lord replied: 'Go back to your place of birth for through me your vision will have a spiritual fulfilment.'[4]

THROUGH DISILLUSION TO TRANSFORMATION

Courage was needed to face up to the implications of this moment. Francis did not persevere in the path which was evidently illusory. The veil had been removed, and he saw it for what it was. His vision was valid, but the interpretation was understood at a deeper level, in a spiritual dimension. So he just got up and returned to Assisi.

He had faced himself, and now he had to face his parents, the people of Assisi, and the misunderstanding, criticism, and perhaps ostracism of his peer group. At this point Celano likens Francis, thrown down and beaten with heavy blows, to Saul on the road to Damascus, and comments on his interior state:

'Francis changes his carnal weapons into spiritual ones and in place of military glory he receives the knighthood of God. Therefore to the many who were astounded at his unusual happiness he said that he was going to be a great prince.'[5]

This seems to be the pilgrimage of Franciscan spirituality, repeated in various ways in the stories of Franciscan saints, and in our own experience. The life stories change, but the spiritual principle remains the same. There is a breaking down of pride, a tumbling off the high horse of arrogance, a realization of the illusion of worldly glory and ambition, and a process of transformation. This takes place through penitence, faith, and a new interpretation of old visions. It is, after all, a gospel principle, and we shall see it repeated in the life of Francis through his conversion, and renewed at every chapter of his experience.

It will become clear to us as we progress, that if we are on the high road of holiness, endeavouring to live out in our own experience the gospel in the light of Francis, we shall also encounter suffering, experience disillusion, and be drawn into an evermore profound level of transformation. It will affect us at every level, from the simplest and earliest evangelical experience of conversion, right through to the deeper reaches of prayer — if we get that far in this life.

THE EXAMPLE OF ST MARGARET OF CORTONA

Such a typical Franciscan experience of transformation through disillusion can be illustrated from brothers and sisters of all three Orders. One of the great tertiaries whose life followed this pattern was St Margaret of Cortona.

She was born in Laviano in 1247. Her father was a prosperous farmer, and when her mother died when she was just seven years old, she was left to run wild.

Two years later her father remarried, but Margaret became restless and unhappy. At seventeen she took a gentleman from Montepulciano as a lover, and for nine years, unmarried and with her illegitimate son, she flaunted herself in the town, ignoring the public scandal she caused.

One significant story tells of her riding on a superb horse, the wind taking her silks and velvets, and the sun catching her jewels, her beauty displayed for all to see. When her servants caught up with her, she remarked how beautiful and peaceful was the hillside and its caves — a place for a hermit to say his prayers. Then she became wistfully silent and lingered there, and was hard to please when she arrived home.

She was sensitive towards the poor, sick, and unhappy, and nursed a reverence for religion, but was shut out by her mortal sin from receiving the sacrament.

One day, in 1274, her lover was found murdered by bandits, and this became the occasion of her conversion. She gave up all his property, showed public penitence for her past, and set out for her father's house in Laviano, but her stepmother rejected the now notorious Margaret.

So, cast out and exhausted, bearing her own grief and her frightened and crying child, she sat down under a fig-tree and comforted the boy through her own tears.

She later recorded the Lord's words to her, recalling the experience:

'Remember, *poverella*, my poor little one, the day when your father, lacking fatherly pity, and urged on by your stepmother, drove you from his house. Not knowing what to do, and being without any adviser or helper, you sat down under a fig-tree in his garden, and there you sought in Me, a Guide, a Father, a Spouse, and Lord; and with a humble heart you confessed your utter misery of soul and body. Then he, the serpent of old, seeing you cast out, sought to his own shame and your destruction, to make your comeliness and youth an inducement to presume upon My mercy; putting it into your heart that, since you were now cast out, you might excusably go into sin, and that you would not lack lovers among the great ones of the world, because of your exceeding beauty. But I, who created the beauty of your soul, and desired again to restore it — I, who loved you still, by My inspiration, enlightened you and admonished your conscience that you should go into Cortona, and put yourself under obedience to my Friars Minor. And you, gathering up your soul, straightway set forth upon the road to Cortona, and there you placed yourself under the care of the brethren, as I had commanded, and with all solicitude you submitted yourself to their counsel and guidance.'[6]

There were times of disappointment and difficulty before her as

31

she moved from disillusion to transformation, but her feet being planted on the way, and in fellowship with the church of San Francesco and the friar Giunta Bevegnati, she proved her conversion by love and compasssion for the poor.

After some years of stringent testing, she was allowed to join the Third Order, and her son, now twelve years old, was accepted by the Arrezzo friars.

Fra Giunta wrote her life and visions after her death, recording many of the trials which she would still undergo, one entry of which reads:

> 'I wish that the example of your conversion should preach hopefulness to those who are despairing, and that it should be to repentant sinners what the morning dew is to plants parched by the sun's heat. I wish that ages to come may be convinced that I am always opening the arms of My mercy.'

One day she recounted some remarkable words which God had spoken to her:

> 'O child, be white with My innocence, and ruddy with My love, for you are the third light granted to the Order of my beloved Francis. He, among the friars, was the first: Clare, among the nuns, was the second: and you, in the Order of Penance, shall be the third.'

After twenty-three years in Cortona, after many trials and in sickness, she died on the day she had foretold, after smiling and saying to those who visited her deathbed: 'The way of salvation is easy, it is just enough to love.'

Both Francis and Margaret learned that the way to transformation was through allowing oneself to be rid of the illusions picked up on the way.

For Francis, it was the destruction and reinterpretation of his early troubadour ambitions, and later a constantly renewed understanding of Christ's word: 'Francis, build my house which you see is falling into ruins.' For us, it may be the destruction of romantic notions of following Christ or living the Franciscan vocation — the taking up of the cross of discipleship in ways we had not bargained for, or thought possible previously.

But always it will be transformation into a new experience of God, a dying to our own insistence of independence and pride, or a more radical interpretation of our own pilgrimage.

If Christ is the true vine and we dwell in him, then his promise is: 'Every branch that bears fruit he [the vinegrower] prunes to make it bear more fruit' (John 15.2). The pattern in that chapter is *fruit* (v.2), *more fruit* (v.2b), and *much fruit* (v.5). The method is pruning, or, as the old version says, purging, and in the mystical tradition this is a pattern which has three stages, *purgation*, *illumination*, and *union*.[7]

We shall look at this pattern of the mystical life later, but a few comments are relevant here. These stages 'come around again' like a spiral staircase that, in retracing itself in a circular manner, actually reaches ever-higher levels. The purgation is an experience of repentance, disillusion, and the demolishing of the old, carnal ways of sin, pride and arrogance, but it leads to flashes of illumination which become more constant as the sanctifying process continues, leading to amazing moments of actual experience of the heavenly life of glory which we call union. It is a transforming union into the life and image of Christ, which plunges us into the divine mystery of God.

If it is the gospel that we are following, then we shall find that this is perfectly compatible with Franciscan spirituality. Indeed, the Franciscan way, and certainly the life of St Francis, is inexplicable apart from the gospel of Christ.

God of my earthly pilgrimage:
Thank you for the divine grace that meets my human need,
  for your constant faithfulness when I lose my vision,
  and for your sustaining strength in times of my weakness.
Enable me to rise from moods of discouragement or despair,
  that renewed in vision and hope, I may continue the journey
  that leads to your eternal love;
Through Jesus Christ my Lord. Amen.

5 ❧ *Evangelical Conversion*

EVANGELICAL AND CATHOLIC

Whatever else we may say about Franciscan spirituality, conversion is basic to its emergence and development. Its beginning is often seen to be sudden, though even in such cases there is found to be a profound and extended period of interior preparation. Evangelical conversion is of this kind, exemplified by the Damascus Road experience of Saul of Tarsus.

But conversion cannot be limited to that period of preparation, with its dramatic faith and enlightenment. The experience may have its beginnings there, but it is prolonged in the whole life of increasing transformation, until the soul reflects the image of God that had been broken and distorted by sin.

This continuing sense of conversion is elucidated by the Benedictine vow of *conversio morum* — what Thomas Merton called the most mysterious of the vows.

> Ultimately this is nothing more and nothing less than commitment to Christ's call to follow him, whatever that may mean. What is certain is that it will involve dying, and not only death at the end of the journey but the lesser deaths in life, the dying to live, the loss which will bring new growth.[1]

Such conversion is obedience and perseverance in the lifelong process of being transformed in the school of Christ.

It is *evangelical* because it is rooted in the Gospels, where Jesus calls: 'Come to me, all you that are weary and are carrying heavy burdens, and I will give you rest.' The response to such a call in repentance and faith is evangelical conversion, which involves forgiveness of sins, a commitment to discipleship, and a personal and intimate fellowship with Christ.

It is *catholic* because it implies the perseverance and continuity of discipleship, growth, progress, and maturity, leading to the ultimate perfection of union with God in love. The invitation of Jesus continues: 'Take my yoke upon you, and learn from me; for I am gentle and humble in heart, and you will find rest for your souls. For my yoke is easy, and my burden is light.'[2]

The tertiary mystic Angela of Foligno, writing of her spiritual pilgrimage, says that she received holy communion regularly *before* she had made confession of her sins or had any sense of God's forgiveness. Being reproached by her conscience and filled with conviction and dread, she prayed that she might be led to a confessor to whom she could unburden her soul. That night St Francis appeared to her and told her that if she prayed sooner the answer would sooner have come.

Next morning, in the church of St Francis, she found a friar preaching — 'whereof I did confess most fully and was absolved of all my sins', she writes. That was but the second of eighteen steps that she enumerates. And only then did she feel that her feet were firmly planted on the mystical path of love for Christ.[3]

Franciscan spirituality builds on the foundation of conversion, in response to the invitation of Jesus in the Gospels, confession of sin leading to a sacramental life within the fellowship of the Church. In Franciscan terms, this involves personal and corporate discipline in which mystical fellowship with Christ brings the pilgrim soul to union with God.

Francis did not produce a system, but lived a life. The next-generation friar Bonaventure also lived the life, but he endeavoured to map the order and progress of spirituality in his major biography of St Francis. He follows the pattern of *purgation, illumination*, and *union (perfection)*, but is careful to warn the reader against systematization without conversion-experience of God:

> I invite the reader to the groans of prayer through Christ crucified, through whose blood we are cleansed from the filth of vice — so that he not believe that reading is sufficient without unction, speculation without devotion, investigation without wonder, observation without joy, work without piety, knowledge without love, understanding without humility, endeavour without divine grace, reflection as a mirror without divinely inspired wisdom.[4]

In the conversion stories of Francis, Jacopone da Todi, and Ramon Lull, the typical Franciscan pattern is expressed in three quite different life-styles, bearing the same family resemblance, and to them we shall now turn.

FRANCIS AT SAN DAMIANO

It is the gospel of grace that leads to conversion in the Franciscan tradition. The call is a divine invitation, and the initiative lies with the Holy Spirit. There is a certain divine imperative in the conversion of Francis. Great souls always feel this to be the case.

Moses was minding his own business and his father-in-law's sheep in the Sinai desert when his curiosity drew him to the bush that burned but was not consumed. Suddenly he was confronted with God, and in trembling and protestation he was faced with the divine imperative and vocation to lead God's people into redemptive freedom.[5]

The word of God came to Jeremiah, saying: 'Before I formed you in the womb I knew you, and before you were born I consecrated you; I appointed you a prophet to the nations.'[6]

Isaiah's famous call and commission came as a result of a vision in the temple, when Isaiah was smitten with the divine holiness to such an extent that there was no option for him but to cry out, after his confession and cleansing: 'Here am I; send me!'[7]

We have already mentioned Saul's Damascus Road experience, which may be placed alongside Francis' conversion, for Francis responded to the same prophetic tradition that Paul later wrote about: 'God, who ... set me apart before I was born and called me through his grace, was pleased to reveal his Son to me.'[8]

John Moorman sees Francis' conversion as a series of divine strokes or visitations by which he submitted to the divine will assaulting his defences and conquering him by grace.[9] This is strong language and high theology, but it does reflect the experience of the prophetic and Franciscan tradition. Human responsibility is also an important factor in conversion, of course, and the voluntary nature of decision and free choice. But there is no contradiction here. It reflects the gospel paradox that runs through a biblical spirituality and is reflected in the Franciscan experience.

The first stroke was when Francis heard the voice in the night at Spoleto when he was all set to follow the cause of knighthood and glory. Despite the risk of being thought cowardly or mad, he returned to Assisi under its compulsion.

The second stroke occurred when Francis was attempting to plunge back into the merry life of parties and festivities with his peer group. He had been elected 'master of the revels', and after feasting the young men were parading through the streets of Assisi with Francis following, wand of office in hand. In the words of his biographer:

All of a sudden the Lord touched his heart, filling it with such surpassing sweetness that he could neither speak nor move. He could only feel and hear this overwhelming sweetness which detached him so completely from all other physical sensations that, as he said later, had he been cut to pieces on the spot he could not have moved.[10]

His companions found him in this trancelike state and came to believe that he was in love — as indeed he was — but not in the way they thought.

The effect of this was that Francis began to withdraw more and more from noise, company and pleasure-seeking, and to spend much time in contemplation and prayer around the countryside and caves of Assisi.

It was at this time that his awareness of the poor deepened into a sensitivity of identification as he made the pilgrimage to Rome and changed places for a day with a beggar. And the incident with the leper led him to spend time and care at the local lazaretto.

All this led up to the third stroke, which completed the initial stage of his conversion before the crucified Saviour.

The small ruined church of San Damiano stood just outside the walls of Assisi. It still had an old priest who said mass at the altar behind which was a painted crucifix in Byzantine style — not a twisted, agonized Jesus, but one whose arms were extended and whose eyes looked out with the invitation: 'Come to me ...' Francis felt prompted to enter, and he knelt before the crucifix and began to pray for clearer guidance in his pilgrimage.

It was then that it happened. Suddenly he was challenged by what seemed to be a voice from the crucified Jesus: 'Francis, go and repair my Church which, as you see, is falling into ruins.'

Trembling and amazed, he answered: 'Gladly I will do so, O Lord.' Certainly there were holes in the roof, decay in the walls, and weeds underfoot. He had truly but not completely understood the words — perhaps it was too much to take in all at once. As Julien Green comments: 'The only mistake lay in that lowercase "c". He should have thought "Church", but how could he have?'[11]

Yet here began a participation in the love and passion of Christ that was to lead him from the first flush of a new love at San Damiano, to the profoundest mystical union with Christ's wounded love at La Verna, for the story says:

> From that hour his heart was stricken and wounded with melting love and compassion for the passion of Christ; and for the rest of his life he carried in it the wounds of the Lord Jesus. This was clearly proved later when the stigmata of those same wounds were miraculously impressed upon his own holy body for all to see.[12]

That same crucifix still hangs in Assisi, though now in the church of Santa Chiara, where the Clares continue their life of prayer. And the conversion of Francis still reverberates down the ages, through the Church and the world, calling us to the same evangelical participation in the passion and glory of Christ.

JACOPONE OF TODI (1230–1306)

Todi lies some twenty miles or so south of Assisi, and there Jacopone was born about six years after the death of Francis. Of an aristocratic family, he studied law in Bologna and became a *notaio*, which included accountancy and law. When he was thirty-eight, he married the beautiful Vanna di Bernadino di Guidone, who had Franciscan penitent sympathies that were certainly not shared by Jacopone.

At Bologna, Jacopone began to appreciate the aesthetic and literary pleasures of creative poetry and music, and on the way became arrogant and self-opinionated, and a connoisseur of food and drink. Bologna's university was only excelled by Paris at that time, and his studies included logic, literature, philosophy, and law. But there he also came into contact with the new poetry, which captured his imagination and stirred up an inward restlessness.

His marriage to Vanna was a match of love, though it must have been difficult for her. He loved to show her off at the social functions they attended around Umbria, in all the finery he encouraged her to wear. But Jacopone's conceit, ambition, and arrogance were belied by the inner restlessness he repressed.

Vanna's beauty and finery hid not only the secret penitence and asceticism of her inward life of love for God, but also the hair shirt which she wore secretly under the beautiful dresses in which she obediently accompanied Jacopone to the social engagements to which they were invited.

Jacopone knew all about Francis, of course. Who could not know of the saint who had been canonized just four years before Jacopone's birth in neighbouring Assisi? The stories of his teaching, miracles, and stigmata were part of the local folklore. There was a Franciscan convent in Todi itself, though the friars there were of the Conventual or *relaxati* type, with a mitigated rule, and not as strict as the *zelanti* or Spirituals who lived especially around Assisi and the Marches of Ancona.

Jacopone had never sorted out their differences, but he did tend to despise the kind of asceticism which was provoked by the emotional processions of flagellants who roamed through the towns of Umbria from time to time, singing and wailing in penitence for the sins of the world. He was especially angered by the young Franciscan hermit Ranieri, who managed to gain converts by a strange ascetic handsomeness and erotic charm.

But what attraction could the crucified Jesus have for Jacopone? It was enough that he attended mass occasionally, as his rank demanded. Strangely, he did find himself sometimes surreptitiously listening to some of the wandering minstrels who sang of their religious hopes and joys in the lauda-type poetry that moved him uncomfortably. Little did he know that later he would himself compose and sing such poetry and music, filled with intensity of emotion, expressing mystical love for the dying and risen Jesus.

Jacopone was, perhaps, afraid of the expression of a love that burns and suffers, and a joy that is filled with pain and longing. For there were hidden and blocked-up feelings that lay dormant within his own soul.

It was less than a year after his marriage that he and Vanna attended a celebration in Todi. He was surrounded by friends and admirers while Vanna went up on to a balcony where the dancers were assembled.

Suddenly the whole structure collapsed, and people fell screaming among the wreckage. There was complete panic as Jacopone ran among the victims and at last found Vanna.

She died in his arms, and as he loosened her bodice to give her air, he discovered the hair shirt. It revealed to him the depth of penitence and love for God that Vanna had always nurtured in her inmost heart. He realized too late that he did not know the woman he had loved.

This was enough to turn Jacopone's mind, and there are many stories of his ensuing madness. There were manic and religious elements in his behaviour over the next few years that in their early manifestations convinced some people that he was completely crazy and revealed to others a certain prophetic symbolism.

He tarred and feathered himself one day and went off to his niece's wedding. Another day he presented himself at the door of St Fortunato Convent in Todi, garbed in a donkey skin, asking to be accepted among the fools of Christ. The *relaxati* friars would have none of it. It was not until ten years after Vanna's death, after spending most of that time in the Third Order, that he was eventually admitted among them.

It was during these intervening years that he undoubtedly visited the Franciscan sites and hermitages, including the chapel at San Damiano, the Portiuncula, and the carceri on Mount Subasio, where he talked with friars of the both groups of Conventuals and Spirituals.

The latter group sought to follow Francis and his Rule quite literally, without gloss or addition. Poverty was the virtue they prized especially. Unfortunately, some of them manifested a negative and judgemental attitude that was not of Francis, and their claims were not always advanced by their filthy condition and extreme ascetic practices.

Among those *zelanti*, nevertheless, Jacopone found genuine Franciscan love and fervour, for friars like the original companions Leo and Rufino lived until 1271, and loved telling the primitive story of Francis, with all his miracles and contradictions that were smoothed over by the *relaxati*.

This latter group were called Conventuals because they not only owned communal property, but had the use of much personal property as well. As time went on, the more lax they became, though among them Jacopone also found good and worthy friars.

These were but emphases and parties within the one Order in Jacopone's day, but eventually it did lead to schism. After years of persecution and strife, the Spirituals, with their later leaders, became established as Observants as distinct from the Conventuals.

As late as 1897, Pope Leo XIII established them, together with the Capuchins, into three separate Franciscan families within the Roman Catholic Church.

Since Jacopone was not at first welcome in the First Order, he became a member of the Third Order. This membership lasted ten years, during which time he became a popular and able preacher of the gospel, with a new sanity and maturity as time passed. He was to be heard and seen in the market-places of Umbria and beyond as he preached and sang the *laudi* that were often set to folksy tunes well loved by the people.

He became one of the classic Franciscan fools for Christ, though even as he deplored the learning of the *litterati* (schoolmen-friars of Paris and Bologna), there is evidence of his own learning and wisdom, which was dedicated to Christ.

He was prepared to be a fool for the Lord, and gloried in that fact. He would preach an emotional and rousing sermon in an Umbrian market-place, and this would be followed by one of the catchy compositions of Jacopone, the refrain echoing a common dance tune:

> *Wisdom 'tis, full joyfully*
> *Crazed for Jesus Christ to be!*

No such learning can be found
In Paris, nor the world around:
In his folly to abound
   Is the best philosophy.

Who by Christ is all possessed
Seems afflicted and distressed,
Yet he's Master of the best
   In science and theology.

Who for Christ is all distraught
Gives his wits, men say, for naught;
Those whom Love has never taught
   Think him foolish utterly.

He who enters this glad school
Learns a new and wondrous rule —
'Who has never been a fool
   Wisdom's scholar cannot be!'

He who enters on this dance
Enters Love's unwalled expanse;
Those who mock and look askance
   Should do penance certainly.

He who wordly praise achieves
Jesus Christ his Saviour grieves,
Who Himself, between two thieves
   On the Cross hung patiently.

He who seeks for shame and pain
Shall his heart's desire attain
All Bologna's lore were vain
   To increase his mastery.

> *Wisdom 'tis, full joyfully*
> *Crazed for Jesus Christ to be!*

As with Francis, the crucified and risen Jesus became the centre of Jacopone's life, preaching, and poetry. One can trace through his spiritual and metaphysical poetry the classic threefold pattern that Bonaventure draws out of the experience of Francis – *purgation*, *illumination*, and *union*. This is the classic mystic way, but it always conforms to the pattern of Jesus. Francis himself could well have written a typical stanza of one of Jacopone's *laudi*:

> For since God's wisdom, though so great
>   Is all intoxicate with love,
> Shall mine not be inebriate,
>   And so be like my Lord above?
> No greater glory can I give
>   Than sharing His insanity.

RAMON LULL (1232–1316)[13]

In a chapel of the church of San Francisco at Palma, Majorca, lie the relics of Ramon Lull, in a cedarwood coffin on which is engraved an epitaph from his own *Tree of Love*:

> Here lies a Lover, who had died for his Beloved, and for love ... who has loved his Beloved with a love that is good, great and enduring ..., who has battled bravely for love's sake ..., who has striven against false love and false lovers ..., a Lover ever humble, patient, loyal, ardent, liberal, prudent, holy and full of all good things, inspiring many lovers to honour and serve his Beloved.

He called himself the 'Fool of Love', and as a Franciscan tertiary he became the 'Apostle of Africa', being also troubadour, poet, missionary, and philosophical theologian.

He was born in Majorca shortly after its liberation from Islamic rule by King James I of Aragon. Large numbers of Moors and Jews lived in Palma, and his mixing with them led to later friendly and religious debate.

At fourteen years of age he became a page at the royal court, and was known as an easy-going and genial fellow, though this attitude led to his later lax morals.

Over the years he learned and composed many troubadour love-lyrics as he fell in and out of love with a number of women. His marriage in his twenties to Blanca Picany, with his two children, made little difference to his philandering. Two stories from that period form the background to his conversion.

In the first he was riding through the city on horseback, and seeing a woman on whom he had had his eye for some time entering a church, he galloped after her, and was only driven out when some irate worshippers came to her aid.

The second story takes up this persistent attitude. The woman, married, and having no desire for his attentions, acted decisively. She agreed to meet him privately, and when he arrived and pestered her with his demands, she turned to him, slowly uncovered her breast, and shocked and frightened Ramon with the sight of a loathsome cancer. 'See, Ramon,' she cried, 'the foulness of this body which has won your affection! How much better had you done to have set your love on Jesus Christ, of Whom you may have a prize that is eternal.'

Looking back years later, he wrote of this period: 'The beauty of women, O Lord, has been a plague and tribulation to my eyes, for because of the beauty of women I have been forgetful of Thy great goodness and the beauty of Thy works.'

But such was the ardent nature of the young Ramon that one summer evening, not long afterwards, when he was thirty years of age, he was composing a love-song to another woman who had taken his fancy. The art of the troubadour was at its height at this time, and he loved turning his hand to a new song — for a new woman.

As he concentrated upon the fine balance of words and rhyme, humming the air to which they would be set, he looked up and gazed abstractedly into space. Then he became aware of being observed.

There, a little to his right, against the wall, as a Catalan biography says, 'was our Lord Jesus Christ hanging upon the Cross', and with great agony and sorrow he looked upon Ramon.

Ramon trembled with fear, dropped his pen, and could neither think nor speak. Trying to evade the gaze of Christ, he threw himself upon his bed, and the vision faded.

Next day, he tried to explain it away in the emotion of the moment, and in the evening took up his pen again. He had hardly begun when the crucified Jesus appeared again, and this time Ramon was even more frightened as he hid his face in his hands to shut out the frightening and persistent vision.

Three times more this happened, causing him to reflect upon the meaning of the experience. There was now no doubt in his mind about the objective nature of the appearances. All the Christian teaching of his boyhood days, accompanied by a powerful conviction of conscience, brought the answer: 'Our Lord God Jesus Christ desired none other thing than that he should wholly abandon the world and devote himself to His service.' Ramon himself records the appearances:

> But Jesus Christ, of His great clemency
> Five times upon the Cross appeared to me,
> That I might think upon Him lovingly,
> And cause His name proclaim'd abroad to be
> Through all the world.

But questions arose. Was he worthy? Could such sins as his be forgiven? Could he, with such opportunities lost and such a carnal life lived, be received into the fellowship of Christ?

He wrestled with these questions through the night, under deep conviction of sin, but by the morning was overwhelmed with 'the great tenderness, patience and mercy which our Lord has toward sinners', and that in spite of his sin, the grace and love of God invited him to dedicate himself to the service of Christ. With the morning, light dawned upon his soul, and:

> Pardon I sought at break of day,
> Contrite and sad, I went straightway
> My sins before God's priest to lay.
>
> Came God's great gifts with hope's glad ray —
> Devotion, love and power to pray —
> And these will ever with me stay.

It wasn't easy. 'Never at any time soever have I experienced such strivings as when I turned from sin to acts of penitence,' he wrote years later. But immediately he turned his mind to study, his heart to prayer, and his hopes to ultimate martyrdom in the proclamation of the gospel.

A public confession and a clean break were called for, and when the newly instituted festival of St Francis was celebrated on 4 October, he was found at mass.

The preacher laid great stress on the completeness of Francis' surrender. He had given up his inheritance, his reputation, his friends and family, and had literally stripped himself naked.

If Ramon had thought to come to terms with the world in his conversion, this clarified the situation. There were no half measures. He returned home, set aside part of his possessions for his wife and children, sold the rest for the poor, and left Majorca to begin a pilgrimage of faith.

This was the beginning of the extended conversion of a long life spent in study, preaching, prayer and solitude, and in writing and debate.

At last, on his final missionary journey in Bugia, North Africa, at eighty-four years of age, he was beaten to death.

FAMILY LIKENESS

These three conversion stories reveal the differences and the family likeness of the typically Franciscan way. Francis was a young man from a merchant class, full of festivity and youthful high spirits. By a series of divine visitations he was brought through restlessness, yearning, and vision of the crucified Jesus, to faith and conversion.

Jacopone was a middle-aged, irreligious connoisseur of foods and wines, a conceited and arrogant lawyer with a beautiful wife and a growing reputation. He was laid low in the dust, and through desolation and madness caused by the loss of his wife, was brought to repentance, peace, and love at the foot of the cross.

Ramon Lull was of noble stock, a young man in the royal court, an unfaithful philanderer and full of romantic love-songs and dissolute living. Without warning, the crucified Jesus pierced him with a look of love and sorrow, until he surrendered to his Beloved and became his fool of Love.

In any framework of Franciscan spirituality, the necessity of conversion is paramount, whether it be instantaneous or over a period of time. The divine initiative indicates the grace and mercy of the crucified Christ, and the necessity of personal repentance and faith indicates the individual responsibility involved at each progressive step.

Such personal conversion is only the beginning, for it opens out into the mystical path of a lifelong pilgrimage. And it immediately becomes sacramental and corporate as the believer grows and matures within the body of Christ and moves out in love and compassion towards a needy world.

But it all begins with the turning of the mind and heart to God in conversion. The cross is the beginning and end of the journey for the Franciscan, and the right note is sounded by Ramon Lull in the prayer which ends this chapter.

When I am wholly confounded, and know not where to look or where to turn, then do Your eyes behold me, and in those eyes which wept for our sins, and that heart which was wounded and cleft for us, do I seek and implore my salvation. And in those tears, and in that love and mercy — there do I find my health and my salvation, and there alone.

6 ✿ *Serving and Building*

CHANGE OF HEART AND LIFE-STYLE

Conversion is no superficial emotional experience in the Franciscan context. There is a rich emotional content in Franciscan spirituality, but the mind is engaged as well as the heart. A new state of feeling and a new direction of will reorientates the believer's life, and faith is expressed in works of compassion and loving service.

The Legend of the Three Companions tells us that just before his encounter with the lepers, Francis was praying fervently, and heard God say:

> O Francis, if you want to know my will, you must hate and despise all that which hitherto your body has loved and desired to possess. Once you begin to do this, all that formerly seemed sweet and pleasant to you will become bitter and unbearable; and instead, the things that formerly made you shudder will bring you great sweetness and content.[1]

It was fair warning. Francis was always aware, when he was clothed in fine and perfumed clothes, and his mind was heady with wine, that there were other sights and smells − the stink of poverty and the stench of leprosy. He would turn his face away, pinch his sickened nostrils in fastidious fear of rotting flesh − but his change of heart produced a change of attitude. 'When I was in sin, the sight of lepers nauseated me beyond measure,' he wrote in his *Testament*, 'but then God himself led me into their company and I had pity of them. When I had once become acquainted with them, what had previously nauseated me became a source of spiritual and physical consolation.'[2]

The early sources picture Francis as the Good Samaritan, washing the lepers' feet, binding up their sores, drawing off the pus, and kissing their wounds. He laid aside his fine clothes, distributed money and food to the poor, increasingly saw the image of Christ in all who suffered, and therefore found himself ministering to Christ as he ministered to them.[3]

Like many a new convert in the first flush of love for Christ, he went over the top. The poor priest at San Damiano's recognized this when Francis brought him the money gained from selling the bales of cloth he had stolen from his father in Foligno, for the priest refused to receive the money.

That first pilgrimage to Rome saw him scatter the whole purseful of (his father's) money before the shrine at St Peter's before he begged alms all day in the exchanged clothes of a smelly beggar. When the sons and daughters of Francis act in dramatic and outrageous ways, they are not altogether responsible, for they are following in the steps of their father, Francis.

BUILDING THE CHURCH OF GOD

Along with the dramatic actions there was a literal quality about Francis' discipleship. The biographers speak of him at this time being drunk with the Spirit, intoxicated with the love of God, and this made him quite impervious to the criticisms and buffetings of the folk of Assisi as they observed what seemed to be increasing madness.

We may well feel some sympathy for Pietro, as Francis' father, when he could control himself no more and dragged his son before Bishop Guido. We don't really know how he felt in his heart when he heard his naked son disown him: 'Until now I called you my father, but from now on I can say without reserve, "Our Father in heaven." He is all my wealth and I place all my confidence in him.'[4]

This seems to have been a necessary launching pad for Francis, and it is worth noting the comments of a recent book on Francis by two Protestant scholars, where a parallel is drawn between the filial separation of Francis from Pietro, and of the young Martin Luther from his father Hans. Both fathers were striving businessmen, social climbers, and wealth-seekers. Both profoundly misunderstood their sons, virulently opposing their religious vocations, not comprehending why a son, nurtured in affluence and headed for success, would reject such security for poverty and celibacy. Both were obedient rebels.[5] And it seemed necessary.

Francis went off into the woods singing, caring neither for local ridicule — nor for the beating given him by some brigands just outside Assisi when he told them that he was the Herald of the Great King.

He then began in earnest his manual work of building that he had learned years before in working on the new wall of Assisi with the stone from the ruined Rocca. But now it was the tumbledown church of San Damiano, then the church of San Pietro, and on to the Benedictine Portiuncula, which was then surrounded by trees but is now within the great Basilica of *Santa Maria degli Angeli*.

This chapel was in a state of ruin at the time, and Francis was especially attracted to it, for its dedication was to the Blessed Virgin Mary, and, as Bonaventure said, it was the place that Francis loved most in the world, and was to become the cradle of the Franciscan movement.

Francis' literal understanding of building the Church of God caused him to beg stones. Between singing the praises of God as a jongleur throughout Assisi, he cried: 'Whoever gives me one stone will have one reward; two stones, two rewards; three stones, a treble reward.'[6] And Celano is quick to point out that though Francis had not yet realized the full implications of what building the Church meant, he was actually already building on the foundation of Christ in his zeal and obedience, 'for other foundation no one can lay, but that which has been laid, which is Christ Jesus'.[7]

As he worked, there were moments of great inspiration, for as one of his early biographers says, he cried out to passers-by one day a prophetic word, in French and Italian: 'Come and help us to do this work for the church of Saint Damian which will become a monastery of women whose life and fame will cause our heavenly Father to be universally glorified.'[8]

AN EVOLVING VOCATION

None of us are able to understand what God wants of us when we first become conscious of the stirrings of his Holy Spirit. Indeed, if we did know, we may well draw back in wonder or in fear.

Many young men and women have been drawn to the Franciscan life by the romantic aura that surrounds those who seem to live in such joy and liberty, having pulled out of the commercial and political rat race. And just as a military uniform has drawn many a young man to the glory and excitement of war, so the Franciscan habit has drawn young men and women to the adventure of the religious life. In both cases there is a rude awakening, for warfare soon reveals its horror and insanity, and the religious life calls the novice ever more deeply into a confrontation between the egocentric self and the searing love of God. And it is not long before the radical demands of the gospel make themselves felt in the life of discipleship.

There is, therefore, an evolution of vocation, and although the cost and fears are different for everyone, there is not only sustaining grace given by God for every need, but a mingling of inspiration and joy as hitherto unrealized potential is brought into play. Let's take an example of a particularly shy and sensitive soul.

Rufino was a gentle and refined man of Assisi who joined Francis in the early days. He spoke very rarely, and had a clear contemplative vocation to prayer and silence. The *Fioretti* makes it clear that he had neither the gift nor the courage to preach, and in any case was afflicted with the impediment of a stammer.

One day Francis told him to go and preach extempore to the people of Assisi. Rufino was greatly distressed and pleaded his inability and ignorance. Francis therefore became adamant and put him under obedience not only to go, but to go stripped to the waist and preach in one of the Assisi churches, because of his reticence.

This terrified Rufino, but he obeyed, and ascended the pulpit and began to stammer somewhat incoherently. The result was that the people began to laugh and jeer: 'Look, they are doing so much penance that they have gone crazy!'

Meanwhile Francis was going through agonies of remorse, and he castigated himself:

'How can you, the son of Peter Bernadone — you vile little wretch — order Brother Rufino, who is one of the noblest citizens of Assisi, to go naked and preach to the people like a madman? By God, I am going to see to it that you yourself experience what you order others to do!'[9]

The *Fioretti* goes on to say that in the fervour of the Spirit Francis stripped as he had commanded Rufino to do, and strode off to Assisi, followed by Brother Leo, who discreetly took along both friars' habits over his arm. The rest of the story concerns the roaring success of the sermon Francis preached, the repentance and conversion of the people, and the joy and reconciliation of the friars.

This is a cameo image of the pain and cost of following a vocation. The level of suffering was very different for Rufino and Francis, or perhaps I should say the *kind* of suffering. They both learned a great deal from the demands of obedience and repentance. But they both learned to enter into joy and wonder as they allowed themselves to be carried into the experience of risk and dread. Brother Leo watched, empathized, understood, and brought about the reconciliation by his very accompanying presence, and by producing the two habits at the right moment.

I am speaking of *vocation*, not in the technical sense of being a monk, nun or friar, but in the basic sense of the *call* of every Christian to be a loving child of God, and of the call of every human being to be more humane — and thus more human. If religion makes you less human, it is bad religion and you are better off without it. And so are your fellows. By this standard, most religious faiths are corrupt — especially when they engender exclusivisms and incite to violence and hatred — even of oneself.

LEARNING ABOUT OURSELVES

The pilgrimage of our evolving vocation sometimes presents us with surprises about ourselves. Take one of the stories of that nobleman of Assisi, Bernard of Quintivalle, who was the first to join Francis.

The sources make much of the fact that the early companions of Francis, following in the way of Christ, rejoiced in shame and insults for his sake. So when Francis sent Bernard to Bologna to preach, Bernard was cursed, beaten, and taunted as a lunatic. He was pushed around, stoned, and dust was thrown into his face. In all this, and much more, he remained patient and joyful, not only enduring, but returning to the public square for several days to face yet more insults and mocking. 'And no matter how much they insulted him, his joyful features always showed that his soul was not troubled.'

Then something happened that really upset him. His holiness and constancy were marked by the people and soon, instead of mocking and insults, he was honoured, and there began a revival of religion, with many converts and a friary established in the city.

Such was the adulation and praise which came his way that he really got frightened and went running back to Assisi and pleaded with Francis to send someone else to Bologna for the sake of the peace and salvation of his soul. 'I am no longer doing any good there,' he said. 'Rather, because of the great honour that is shown me, I am afraid of losing more than I would gain.'[10]

We learn a great deal about ourselves in the unfolding of our vocation. We begin by building our churches of stones and mortar, and then gradually realize that the temple of God consists of living stones and is to be a fit dwelling place for the Holy Spirit.[11]

Our material and manual work become a labour of loving fellowship, and the building process becomes a network of compassionate relationships, irradiated by the divine presence.

For Francis, the threefold Order of sisters and brothers became a community of love and a prototype for the whole world in which God is Father, exercising his paternal and maternal care in the world of sisters and brothers. This vision embraces the whole cosmic order. But it must begin with a literal following of the gospel word: 'Francis, go and repair my Church which, as you see, is falling into ruins.'

O God of love and mercy:
You have called me into the fellowship of love and service,
and I have taken the first steps along the way;
As the implications of my vocation widen and deepen my
perspective, so give me the grace and vision to keep on
following.
Forgive me for being slow to understand, and stubborn in my
obedience;
Remove my cowardice of heart and grant that I may trust you
in the dark places, and rejoice in your sustaining love;
Through Jesus Christ my Lord. Amen.

7 🐾 *Community of Love*

PERSONAL AND COMMUNITY VOCATION

'When God gave me some friars,' wrote Francis in his *Testament*, 'there was no one to tell me what I should do; but the Most High himself made it clear to me that I must live the life of the Gospel.'[1] This simple statement makes clear three things. First, that Francis had a profound inward sense of his own vocation; second, that the development within that personal vocation moved towards community; third, that the pattern of this community was that of Jesus and his disciples — the pattern of the gospel.

God has no grandchildren within the Franciscan family. The primary mark of a Franciscan vocation is that the brother or sister is a son or daughter of God, unconditionally loved, called by name, saved by grace, and valued for his or her own personal worth.

This does not mean that there are not times of loneliness and darkness. In fact, the people who are entrusted with periods of desolation and aridity are those who plumb the depths of the dark side of the human condition. Part of their vocation is that they confront this dimension for themselves and for all those who never pray. But there is always this knowledge of being marked, moved, chosen, and irresistibly drawn by the divine Love.

This is true for every Christian, of course, but because so many have become immune to the gospel by a familiarity with the words, the story of Francis brings the gospel into focus again. It is a new birth into the life of God. Being born again is not the monopoly of an exclusivist and dogmatic fundamentalist group. *All* God's people are born again, and the powers of the new birth are intensely personal, as the Holy Spirit moves within the human heart.

We tend to think of the Holy Spirit's ministry primarily through things religious — the preaching of the word and the celebration of the sacraments, neglecting the dimension of the created order. In the Nicene Creed, the Holy Spirit is 'the Lord and giver of life', bringing nature and grace together in divine harmony, and many people encounter the Holy Spirit in nature before they discern his call in Scripture and sacrament.

Such an experience may begin in early childhood, as it did with me. Before I could put a name to it, there was that strange, cosmic movement of the divine in earth, sea, and sky. It was a *felt* mystery that called out to me in creation and demanded my inward response. I heard it in the sighing of the wind, in the movement of the tides, in the waxing and waning of the moon, and in the cycle of the seasons.

At twelve years of age, it became distinctly religious as I gladly and tearfully responded to a definite and personal call to Christ as Saviour, Friend, and Brother. But before that, it was none the less the divine Spirit moving in the created order.

There should be no *separation* between nature and grace, though there may be a *distinction* for the sake of description. The energies of God are shot through the whole of creation, and that is why some people feel God's loving presence and inspiration in nature before they acknowledge it in grace.

Anything good, true, and beautiful may communicate the divine presence, and (apart from sin) even the sad and melancholy experiences of life may echo in our own depths and indicate our need to embrace the creative love of God. It may be art, poetry, music, or sculpture. It certainly is reflected in the whole spectrum of human relationships, for they may lead us to the loving heart of God.

We have seen that Francis' love of nature was rooted in his childhood, and during his sickness following his imprisonment in Perugia, his soul was desolate because he had lost that profound sense of mystic communication as he gazed out over the plain of Umbria — he was lonely for God.

Nature and grace ran together gloriously as he was faced with the crucified and risen Christ in the San Damiano crucifix, and as he embraced the suffering Christ in the lepers at the *Lazaret San Lazzaro d'Arce*, a mile or two outside Assisi.

Personal disillusion and disappointment mingled with the upsurge of an inward vocation to God as his vision became clearer. The working out of such a dramatic and personal sense of vocation was to take the whole of Francis' life, as it does for all of us. It was not a clear and distinct transition from the personal to the communal. The tensions and paradoxes of the hermit and the preacher were to mingle in the progressively unified life of Francis up to his death. This seems to be common in the Franciscan tradition, as much with tertiaries as with the first two Orders.

Sad deformations of the Franciscan life are brought about when sisters and brothers are not allowed the freedom and discipline to develop their personal vocation in the mystical life, for their creative energies may be exhausted in frenetic communal activities within and outside the convent or friary. To find oneself wholly, there has to be an abandonment to the divine Love and the progressive experience of union with God. Ramon Lull expresses this in his *Book of the Lover and the Beloved*:

Whether Lover and Beloved are near or far is all the same, for their love mingles as water mingles with wine. They are joined as heat is with light. They agree and are as closely united as Essence and Being.

The Lover said to his Beloved, 'You are all, and through all, and in all, and with all. I will have you wholly that I may have, and be, myself wholly.' The Beloved answered, 'You cannot have me wholly unless you are mine.' And the Lover said, 'Let me be yours wholly, and you be mine wholly.'[2]

It is only as the individual grows in personal maturity and self-acceptance that he or she is able to relate to others in openness and love. This was certainly true of Francis, but there is a very sad and significant comment in the *Legend of the Three Companions* that sheds some light on Francis' relationship with his father Pietro. The context is Francis' increasing asceticism and deprivation before he is joined by companions:

When his father saw him in this pitiful plight, he was filled with sorrow, for he had loved him very dearly; he was both grieved and ashamed to see his son half dead from penance and hardships, and whenever they met, he cursed Francis.[3]

Murray Bodo picks up this fragment and changes a few words to indicate the reciprocal attitude of Francis to his father:

When Francis saw Pietro's miserable plight, he was very sad, for he loved him dearly; he was grieved and ashamed to see his father half dead from his obsession with money and power. And when he met his father in the bishop's piazza, he renounced him publicly.[4]

We have already spoken of the filial separation of father and son which may have been necessary in the maturing and sharpening of Francis' vocation. But it is also an indication of the similarity of temperament shared by Pietro and Francis — both dramatic, fiery, violent, and stubborn. Therefore, neither could give way. The 'Pica' side of Francis is seen as the *Legend* comment continues. As Francis is berated by Pietro's curses, he takes a vagrant as his father, saying:

'Come with me and I will give you the alms I receive; and when I hear my father cursing me, I shall turn to you saying: "Bless me, Father"; and then you will sign me with the cross and bless me in his place.' And when this happened, the beggar did indeed bless him; and Francis turned to his father, saying: 'Do you not realize that God can give me a father whose blessing will counter your curses?' Many people, seeing his patience in suffering scorn, were amazed and upheld him admiringly.[5]

Bodo is certainly moved by this episode, and makes the point that if Francis had remained rejected and despised he may have eventually come to his father and begged his forgiveness, asking him to understand the sincerity of his decision to serve God alone. But once he became *Il Santo*, Assisi's saint, then such an approach would only have further humiliated his father, making him an object of pity for failing to recognize how great a prophet Francis really was. Bodo's own contemporary Franciscan spirit is evident when he writes:

> I want to believe that a secret reconciliation did take place, that Francis comforted his dying father and received his blessing; but that is likely only something inside myself that needs it to have happened that way. Experience and the testimony of his chroniclers tell me that it was otherwise: that the Gospel divides families, that mothers lose their sons because of their husbands, and sons reject their fathers because of their own call to be themselves, to be different from the one who engendered them. And God's face becomes the face of what each one wishes secretly could have happened, had not pride or circumstances or life itself made it impossible.[6]

I have told my own story of the moving experience that took place between my father and myself just before he died.[7] My father was frail, blind, and withdrawn, and only wanted to be visited by the immediate family. I took him in a wheelchair to St James' Park in Swansea, and as we sang and prayed together with a certain shared sadness and loneliness, we were able to confess that we loved one another – not without tears. This is my last real and abiding memory of him, and one for which I am grateful to God.

Perhaps the memory of Pietro was Francis' secret thorn in the flesh that he carried in sadness but which enabled him to open himself completely to divine and human love in every other relationship. His overwhelming influence down the centuries is one that promotes reconciliation and healing in all human and creaturely relationships. And that brings us back to that sacred moment which launches him into a new family — the beginnings of the Franciscan Order.

THE FRIARS MINOR

Having burned his bridges between his family and himself, there may have been much sorrow and heart-searching and a certain loneliness as Francis set out in his hermit garb to bind up the lepers' sores and build the ruined churches around Assisi. But because his personal vocation was rooted in the divine call, he could not help, in troubadour style, to tell and sing of the goodness and love of God.

The link between his personal and communal vocations can be seen in his response to the reading of Scripture. On the Feast of St Matthias in the year 1209, Francis listened to the reading of the mass Gospel at the Portiuncula and received the revelation of his vocation as mendicant friar:

> 'Go, proclaim the good news. "The kingdom of heaven has come near." Cure the sick, raise the dead, cleanse the lepers, cast out demons. You received without payment; give without payment. Take no gold, or silver, or copper in your belts, no bag for your journey, or two tunics, or sandals, or a staff; for labourers deserve their food. Whatever town or village you enter, find out who in it is worthy, and stay there until you leave. As you enter the house, greet it. If the house is worthy, let your peace come upon it ... '[8]

Francis trembled with joy and cried out with a new enthusiasm: 'This is what I wish, this is what I am seeking, this I long with all my inmost heart to do.' So he threw away his staff, his shoes, and his cloak, keeping only a tunic, replacing his leather girdle with a cord. Celano says that he immediately began preaching repentance, forgiveness, and peace with extempore words that were like a burning fire, and he seemed to his hearers as one transformed.[9]

The elements of peace and joy were uppermost in his preaching. Unlike many of the heretical reformers and sects of his time, he did not curse or insult, but commended the grace of God with humility, courtesy, and assurance. This was what drew people to him, and soon he was joined by companions.

The second significant reading of Scripture took place when his first two followers, Bernard of Quintivalle and Peter Catanii, accompanied Francis to the church of San Nicole to hear mass. They did something which seemed to become a habit with Francis in later years – opening the Bible at random, expecting to find God's guidance in the word of Scripture.

They opened the missal the first time and read: 'If you wish to be perfect, go, sell your possessions, and give the money to the poor.' The second time they read: 'Take nothing for your journey.' And the third: 'If any want to become my followers, let them deny themselves, and take up their cross and follow me.'

'O Brothers,' said Francis, 'this is our life and rule, and the life and rule of all those who may wish to join us. Go therefore, and act on what you have heard.'[10] And they did!

THE OBJECTIVE NATURE OF FRANCIS' VOCATION

Francis was aware of the dangers of subjectivity. He knew that if this was the beginning of a gospel community (and he did not then envisage a monastic order), then there was need to be under the discipline and authority of Scripture in the fellowship of the greater Church.

His preaching was not meant to be the interior visions of a charismatic personality, but the gospel of Christ in its fullness. He did not want such a community to be bound in any legalistic or religious manner, but that adherence to gospel simplicity and poverty should be its hallmark. As he made clear to Cardinal Hugolino (the future Pope Gregory IX), when the numbers had run into thousands:

> My brothers, God called me to walk in the way of humility and showed me the way of simplicity. I do not want to hear any mention of the rule of St Augustine, of St Bernard, or of St Benedict. The Lord has told me that he wanted to make a new fool of me in the world, and God does not want to lead us by any other knowledge than that.[11]

Francis was convinced of the objective nature of his vocation, as St Paul was of his, evidenced in the letter to the Galatians. But when the friars became twelve in number, Francis decided it was time to get approval, confirmation, and direction from the pope. This decision brought with it the courage to make a direct appeal, so that Francis' life and preaching could be recognized as orthodox and distinct from the warring sects such as the Cathari and Waldensians.

Pope Innocent III gave his verbal assent to Francis' Gospel Rule in 1209, to the surprise of many. The pope seemed to have had a dream in which he saw the Lateran basilica tottering on its foundations until propped up by a small insignificant friar who was evidently Francis. This gave Francis the approval, recognition, and freedom of movement he needed to spread the life and teaching throughout the world.

A modern biographer writes of the great building which rose upon this simple but firm foundation:

> Within a period of slightly more than five years, Francis had progressed from being the lone builder of a single chapel outside Assisi to becoming a recognized renewer of the church throughout Italy. A builder is a reconciler and perfector of varied materials. He fits together wood and stone, lime and clay, taking disparate items and forming them into an overarching unity. Francis as a builder brought together nobles and peasants, knights and townsmen, men and women, to form a movement for church renewal that would spread throughout Christendom and incorporate some 30,000 persons by the end of the thirteenth century. People of varying perspectives, divergent nationalities, different educations, and of many vocations were drawn to the man and his movement, catching his vision of a church renewed and restored, reborn and revitalized. Enormous energies would be released and multitudes would be mobilized by the call Francis felt he had received from Christ to 'go rebuild my church'.[12]

INTERNATIONAL COMMUNITY OF LOVE

We have seen that Francis was not attracted to the old monastic foundations, many of which were decrepit and lax. He did not want choir monks and lay brothers, or terms like Master, Abbot, or Prior. His was a fellowship of love – brothers, soon to be joined by sisters, and then Third Order families who would live in humility, love, and joy, imbued by gospel principles, caring for one another, and allowing that care to overflow in compassionate service in the world. And the typical Franciscan greeting would be: 'The Lord give you peace.'[13]

When I was a novice at our friary in Dorset, one Christmas time we put on a concert and party for the village people, with scenes from the life of St Francis. I remember the enactment of Francis listening to the priest reading the mass Gospel at the Portiuncula.

Our Brother Samuel was taking the part of Francis, and I remember well the light and joy on his face as he cried out: 'This is what I wish, this is what I am seeking, this I long with my inmost heart to do.'

Sam is now Guardian of that friary, and we often share fellowship in the love and joy of Christ. This scene from the life of Francis always brings his face and voice before me.

Francis was neither subjective in his vision nor parochial in his outreach, for right back in those early days with the first few brothers, he announced a prophetic vision which Celano records:

> I saw a great multitude of men coming to us and wanting to live with us in the habit of our way of life and under the rule of our blessed religion. And behold, the sound of them is in my ears as they go and come according to the command of holy obedience. I have seen, as it were, the roads filled with their great numbers coming together in these parts from almost every nation. Frenchmen are coming, Spaniards are hastening, Germans and Englishmen are running, and a very great multitude of others speaking various tongues are hurrying.[14]

Lord Jesus Christ:
By your Holy Spirit you called your servant Francis to live according to the simplicity of your holy Gospel, and gave him the vision of a community of love;
Grant that we, drawn by the same Spirit, and following in his footsteps, may share in that community and be touched by the divine fire;
For your dear name's sake. Amen.

8 ❧ *The Evangelical Counsels*

THE THREE VOWS

Decision, commitment, vows. These are part of the response to the call of Christ. Indeed, there is only one vow, and that is taken gladly, joyfully, exuberantly, out of a penitence that has been transformed into love in the light of the cross. It is a vow of dedication to Christ as Saviour and Lord, a vow which includes the whole of life and embraces eternity:

> High heaven that heard the solemn vow
> That vow renewed shall daily hear;
> Till in life's latest hour I bow
> And bless in death a bond so dear.

There is nothing dutiful or legalistic about it — it is a free response to a free gift of love, a reciprocated commitment, the sign of a divine covenant sealed with the blood of Christ. As such, it belongs to all the people of God, and is entered into by conversion and baptism, and is continually renewed and enjoyed in the sacrament of the Eucharist.

Monastic vows began in the same way. They too were a full and free response to the call of God, and in the Franciscan tradition this had to do with penitence, faith, and the joy of conversion.

The threefold monastic commitment was derived from the gospel. The vows were poverty, celibacy (or chastity), and obedience, and were thought of as the evangelical counsels. They were an overflow of response to the life and teaching of Jesus, and though they were somewhat adapted to the Third Order, the same threefold response was in evidence.

For the First and Second Orders, poverty meant literally owning nothing, personally or communally; celibacy meant surrendering all specifically sexual relationships; obedience meant accepting the will of God as expressed in the community. These were relevant to the Third Order as single and married people living in the world, though chastity is a better word than celibacy in most cases.

Poverty is a simplification of life, defining an attitude to money, life-style, and the whole natural environment. Chastity indicates not only the way in which married people relate to one another, but the whole gamut of human relationships and the consecration of one's sexuality within a creative response to the world. Obedience reveals an openness to God and to one's fellows in which there is a patterned order — spontaneity and discipline running together in an integrated harmony.

St Francis' conversion coincided with the beginning of the thirteenth century, when the monastic tradition, as the wider Church, was in decay. There was not only a deterioration in faith and morals in which the carnal world was embraced, but paradoxically a dualistic puritanism in which the good world was denied. By that I mean that personal poverty had allowed the monk to enjoy an excess of luxury through communal surfeit. The monk was not married, but there was often lax sexual morality, and if not, then gluttony and laziness. Obedience became more and more a monastic contrivance than an expression of the will of God.

There were notable exceptions, of course, but as Omer Englebert says, it would be to deceive oneself to see in the end of the twelfth and beginning of the thirteenth centuries a sort of Golden Age. There were hospitals for the sick, abbeys of monks, and churches, pilgrimages, and crusades,

> But if one remembers that these hospitals, these cathedrals and these monasteries were often built for repentance as a penance by the grand wrongdoers to expiate their violence and their crimes; if one recalls that heresy and lust and general incontinence of manners infected Christianity, and that the humbler people were never more the victims of social injustice, one must conclude that the times of St Francis give place to no others in scandal and calamity.[1]

It was into this kind of a world that Francis preached the poverty that relinquishes material gain and shares everything as a joyful mendicant. Here he lived out a chastity that, far from manipulating others to his own use, opened up reciprocal relationships that enabled him to eat from the same bowl as a leper and invite Clare to a meal at the Portiuncula in which they were both caught up in the flame of the divine Love. And here, in this world of violence and power structures, he offered his life in obedience to God first, and in humble service to the rest of creation.

It will be painful for us to look more closely at his vowed life, for its pure and brilliant light will cause our sore eyes to weep over our own sins and over a dying world. But the result will be, as is always the case in the Franciscan adventure, to cause us to add our small light to his, so that the darkest places of our world may be the brighter.

VOLUNTARY POVERTY

The poverty that Francis espoused was not the sort that crushed human beings into a trap of deprivation. It was rather a voluntary identification with the poor in which they are enriched. His period was one in which the rural economy was giving way to market centres and a mercantile economy that eventually was to dominate, develop, and plunder the earth of its non-renewable resources. He rejected his father's kind of capitalism. His life-style was a rebuke to the accumulation of wealth and a rejection of class based on money, property, and power.

His reverence and intimate feeling for all life freed him from ownership, and his relation with the earth was not utilitarian, but one of gratitude and praise for God's bounty. Behind all this was a sense of co-operative fellowship with the earth rather than the dominating will to subdue nature.

Neither is this attitude one which sees voluntary poverty as an end in itself. It is a gospel principle which follows the life of Jesus and enters more intimately into the life of God. Confronted with such radical Franciscan discipleship, possibilities of new perspectives open up that redefine the purpose and experience of personal and communal life.

This is demonstrated in the first companion who turned to Francis — Bernard of Quintivalle, and in the reaction-response of the grasping priest Sylvester, who became one of the most humble and prayerful friars.

After hearing the gospel words: 'If you will be perfect, go and sell what you have and give to the poor, and come, follow Me,' Francis, Peter Catanii, and Bernard set up a distribution point to give away Bernard's wealth and possessions.

As they were thus engaged, Sylvester came up and addressed Francis: 'You did not pay me all you owe for those stones you bought to repair the churches.' The *Fioretti* reports that Francis, marvelling at Sylvester's greed, put his hand into Bernard's cloak, and, filled with money, opened it into Sylvester's lap. 'If you ask for more, I will give you still more,' he said. But Sylvester retreated, perhaps shamefacedly, with the money.

That evening he was seized with reproach of himself, and shaken by the fervour and holiness of the friars. This lasted for three days and nights, and ended in his disposing of all his property. 'Later he became a Friar Minor,' reports the *Fioretti*, 'and was so holy and filled with grace that he spoke with God as one friend to another.'[2]

Francis' call coincided with the emergence of the moneyed merchant class in which self-esteem and rank in society would be measured in proportion to the acquisition of wealth. Money, and what it represents, increasingly became the aim of life, and we seem to have come full circle now in our modern Britain-within-Europe in which all our lives seem geared to market forces. This ideology has invaded our values of self-worth, health, education, food-production, and commerce.

In the Church, like the priest Sylvester, we are confronted by the fearful and blazing light of Francis. We can either turn away like the rich young man faced by Jesus' radical demand, or allow the Franciscan light to dispel our avaricious darkness as Sylvester did.

It was not that Francis was a social reformer or an ideological politician warning what love of money would do to the fabric of our society. Rather, he was a follower of Jesus who saw what it would do to spiritual awareness and sensitivity.

The compulsive worship of capital leads the individual and society to a denial of the compassion that relinquishes more than is necessary and shares in simplicity.

It is all there in the gospel. Jesus preached and lived such radical simplicity clearly, and Francis showed it could be done. But no doubt we shall find ways to evade them both!

CELIBACY/CHASTITY – THE WAY TO LOVE

I have a transistor radio in my hermitage, and tuning in recently I heard a current pop song by Sandy Posy: 'A single girl needs a sweet loving man to lean on . . .' – and I said: 'Well Sandy, I hope you find one!' It is the story of our human condition – we all need love. The words celibacy and chastity are not opting-out words, but inclusive words if we understand them aright.

The monastic tradition has often erred in denying special friend-ships between men and women, fearing lest there be a compromise of chastity. To live in such a negative way produces people who are sexually cold, and no longer capable of open, loving, joyful relationships. Fortunately, the tradition gave more heed to the gospel than to its own legalistic rules with its built-in dualism, so frequently friendship, love, and openness flowered without offending true chastity.

The Franciscan tradition illustrates this. Francis was aware of the cramping style of monasticism once it was legalized and put into rules and constitutional, organized form. That was why he found it so difficult to compose a Rule other than a few sentences from the Gospels with inspirational extempore comment.

He was quite clear about sexual chastity. It meant abstinence for brothers and sisters of the First and Second Orders, and discipline within marriage for Third Order brothers and sisters. But this was not a negative retreat into an asexual frigidity when relating to other human beings. In one of the few extant writings of Francis, he speaks tenderly to Brother Leo, who had been feeling lonely:

> As a mother to her child, I speak to you, my son. In this one word, this one piece of advice, I want to sum up all that we said on our journey, and, in case hereafter you still find it necessary to come to me for advice, I want to say this to you: In whatever way you think you will best please our Lord God and follow in his footsteps and in poverty, take that way with the Lord God's blessing and my obedience. And if you find it necessary for your peace of soul or your own consolation and you want to come to me, Leo, then come.[3]

In our own day we are aware that sexuality is not limited to its genital expression. We know that *all* our relationships, all our creativity, inspiration, and appreciation of things good, true, and beautiful are suffused by our sexuality, which lends warmth, tenderness, and enchantment. Francis and his company may have shared the inhibitions of his day, but *practically*, there was a joyful celebration of human relationships.

Celibacy, in such a context, is not a denial of sexuality, but a way of sharing that has not only an intellectual, but also an emotional and tender dimension. It can be a freedom from narrow, exclusive relationships, so that powerful sexual energy may be transmuted into spiritual sharing and appreciation. All this involves discipline as well as spontaneity, but to forgo human loving because of the risks involved is a poor sort of existence.

The so-called sexual freedom of the swinging sixties and the liberated seventies looked very different from the vantage point of the eighties, with sexual satiety on the one hand and the horror of AIDS on the other.

The nineties have already made sexual chastity and abstinence a real and positive option. It is possible today to hear people speak of a preference for celibacy, whereas in the eighties such folk would be thought to be psychologically odd, or making a virtue out of necessity!

None of this denies the very real value and normality of a full-blooded, sexually active married life in which the experience of sexual encounter, adventure, and pilgrimage are shared, and the joys of parenthood and family are seen as a gift of God.

But much has been preached and written about marriage and the family, and it is necessary to speak of the joys of a single life, the emotional energies, time, and money available for sharing in a gospel and Franciscan style. If marriage is to be celebrated within the Christian family (and it should be!), then so must the joys and opportunities of a single life. After all, it is the pattern of Jesus, Paul, and many of the apostles. And both patterns are alive and well in the Franciscan tradition.

Let me be a bit mischievous, and quote here the first paragraph of an excellent chapter on sex in Robert Van de Weyer's *The Way of Holiness*:

> Monks are no less susceptible to the sin of envy than the rest of us. So when they look over the monastery wall at their married friends in the world, they are inclined to imagine that every couple enjoys a passionate and pleasurable sexual relationship. Yet equally many married people look enviously towards the monastery, jealous of the freedom from sexual anxiety which monks appear to enjoy.[4]

I just mentioned the spiritual transmutation of sexual energy into spiritual channels of love and service. That sounds somewhat ethereal and idealistic, so let me make it plain in human experience. When I wrote the story of Jacopone da Todi, I was very conscious that when his beautiful young wife Vanna fell to her death after less than a year of marriage Jacopone always carried a yearning for her love within his heart. He never looked at another woman sexually because of Vanna, and after ten years as a Franciscan tertiary he entered the First Order friary at Todi.

I picture him on his pilgrimage to Mount La Verna as he turns over in his mind the discipline of the three vows in the lax *mitigati* convent of San Fortunato:

> He rejoiced in the first vow of poverty — but desired much greater stringency than was possible in a convent of the *mitigati* rule. Obedience was the vow which made him wince. It was not that he wished to move out of God's will, but ecclesial obedience did not, for Jacopone, always

seem to coincide with what he believed was God's will!

And celibacy. He was not tempted with the kind of lust that had driven some friars to secret sexual encounters with certain local women who seemed to have a fascination for men under vows! And he had no preference for those of his own sex.

But there were times when he thought of Vanna – when he longed for the touch of a woman's hand, not only in physical embrace but in wifely comfort. He remembered with a smile the feeling that engulfed him when he was clothed in his new habit at his profession in vows. Margarita had made it for him and he supposed that she had 'put love in every stitch'.

He also remembered the day, not so long ago, when he had allowed himself to face up to, and admit, his feelings of deprivation because of the lack of a woman's touch. Why was it that he had been so long in honestly admitting this? 'I am certainly deprived,' he acknowledged as he strode along the road. 'I feel it in physical need, in emotional warmth and in a hunger of spirit that causes me an aching yearning which nothing else seems to satisfy or assuage. Yes, I am deprived. But what of it? God calls me to remain alone and He knows it is sometimes almost impossible.'

There had been times of wandering in the hills above Todi when he had felt God offer him the way of marriage and family again. And then, as if to complicate or negate the offer, the Lord would seize him in such inebriation of spirit that he would cry out in joy – rolling or dancing before the Lord for gladness of heart, and often with tears. At such times he would cry out: 'Have your own way, O Lord, for therein is my peace.'[5]

This is an example of the transmutation in action. It does not entirely dispel loneliness and even a certain sense of deprivation. But married and single men and women have their own joys and their own crosses to bear, and if we can see human love within the context of the creative love of God, then that will cause us to find our *ultimate* peace and rest in God alone.

OBEDIENCE – A WAY OF LISTENING

Perhaps it's because I'm a Celt, but I've always found difficulty with obedience, and even more so when I was Guardian in a Franciscan house where the buck stopped with me!

71

Perhaps I find it easier to write about, because in a chapter on obedience from my hermitage, I said:

> There is a threefold monastic vow: poverty, chastity (or celibacy) and obedience. Poverty is not negative penury but the desire to own nothing, sharing a simple life, and is a gospel witness in a materialistic society. Celibacy is not coldness but the desire to consecrate the profound depths of love and sexuality to God and to people while surrendering a specific genital relationship. This is a relationship witness in a sex-obsessed society. Obedience is the surrender to God's will directly, through the Spirit's voice in scripture and community. This is a disciplined witness in a self-orientated society.[6]

That sounds fine, but it is not quite so simple! Poverty and celibacy are difficult enough, though there is great joy in their positive fulfilment. But obedience is more difficult, and sometimes complicated, for the 'will of God' is not always clear.

In any case, the very notion of a vowed obedience seems a contradiction to my rebellious and independent temperament. I will render obedience to no man or woman, because personal freedom is the basis of corporate liberty. Is this the way for a friar to talk?

Obedience needs defining, for that is where the problem lies, and there is all the difference between obedience to a legalistic command and the response to free grace.

The kind which makes my hackles rise is *slavish obedience* commanded by a tyrant or overlord with penalties for refusal, whether secular or religious. It is a moral duty to *resist* such totalitarian demands and regimes. Think of the apostle Peter's reply to the religious authorities when they forbade him to witness to Christ: 'We must obey God rather than any human authority' (Acts 5.29).

Military obedience I cannot grant. There can be no conditional obedience to a military command in wartime — it has to be unconditional. Otherwise the force would be in disarray, giving the battle to the enemy. Military training and practice based on unquestioning obedience can lead to the idea of 'my country right or wrong', which was voiced both by a military general and a cardinal during the Vietnam War! The dangers are obvious.

Then there is *legal obedience*, which is lawful and sensible, though irksome. The law-making process compels us to common assent for the greater good, and is dutiful rather than joyful, but is necessary in any civilized society.

Wisdom obedience is the counsel of a guru, master, or teacher who leads the initiate or novice into maturity and perfection, and this carries its own justification. It applies to the moral life, to an art or craft, to athletic training or spiritual pilgrimage. This is what was practised in the Franciscan tradition in the early days (though deteriorating later), and is still part of the traditional way. It may also include warning-counsel if you do not obey, but this is not punishment, but chastisement and correction, just as a loving parent will discipline the child in love, though it is not appreciated at the time (Heb. 12.5–13)!

This brings us to *loving obedience*, which is the essence of the gospel. It is a call to harmonize with the will of God, which is joyfully perceived and assented to by the hearer. All the commands of Jesus are of this kind and issue in forgiveness, rest, peace, hope, illumination, and joyful service. In a word, salvation. The great invitation of 'Come to Me' in Matthew 11.28–30 clearly illustrate this.

The word *obedience* comes from the Latin root *audire* – to hear, to listen. The prefix, making it *ob-audire*, signifies *instant and alert listening*, so that the mind and heart are given to the action. This is the way Jesus listened and learned obedience to the Father (Heb. 5.7–9). True obedience is not a slavish assent to an external command, it is rather a loving, and so at times a suffering, response to the love of God. And only love can answer love.

FRANCISCAN OBEDIENCE – A MIDDLE WAY

One of the dangers of the great multiplicity of stories in the Franciscan writings is that it is possible to be selective in a biased manner. You can choose 'obedience stories' like the one in which Francis describes the truly obedient friar under the figure of a corpse that has no will of its own.[7] Some find this enlightening – I find it chilling! It is comforting to discover that the next story Celano relates says that a command under obedience should rarely be given, for in a rash superior such power to command is a sword in the hand of a madman!

There is a story from the seventeenth-century friar Luke Wadding in which a brother would not submit to the discipline of obedience. Francis placed him in a pit and got the friars to bury him up to his chin. 'Are you dead, brother?' asked Francis. The humble reply came (who can blame him?): 'Yes, father, or at least I deserve to die for my sins.' So Francis ordered the friars to dig him out again and set him upon his obedient way.[8]

Perhaps this should be taken as a Zen story, in the same way as that of the two novices who were commanded by Francis to do what he did as he planted cabbages with their roots in the air. (I've been thinking of this as I've been planting cabbages this week.) One imitated Francis, and the other protested. You can guess the rest of the story — or can you? Bartholomew of Pisa said that the upside-down novice was commended and the other dismissed. But I think that Francis, in certain moods, would have commended the other and recognized his initiative. Obedience is a peculiar thing!

If I were to choose my favourite story, it would be the one where Francis told Brother Stephen to prepare certain foods for the kitchen one day, and on the next day to prepare nothing.

Then when Francis found that there was no food, he chided Stephen, who protested that he had been acting under obedience. Francis replied: 'Dear son, discretion is a noble virtue nor should you always fulfil all that your superior bids you, especially when he is troubled by any passion.'[9] You pays your money and you takes your choice!

FRANCISCAN RADICALISM TODAY

In the *Legend of the Three Companions* there is a mind-blowing paragraph that turns the world upside down, and starkly portrays the radical nature of Francis' understanding of the gospel:

> The Bishop received Francis with kindness but said: 'It seems to me that it is very hard and difficult to possess nothing in the world.' To this blessed Francis replied: 'My Lord, if we had any possessions we should also be forced to have arms to protect them, since possessions are a cause of disputes and strife, and in many ways we should be hindered from loving God and our neighbour. Therefore in this life we wish to have no temporal possessions.'[10]

How can we as Christians and Franciscans possibly come to terms with such an attitude? And should we? Consider these questions with me:

Poverty

In my personal life, am I expected to share all my money and goods that are superfluous to an extremely simple life-style? Wouldn't this mean that I would have no bank account, pay no insurance, have no mortgage, own no property? What about my family, and the demands of spouse and children? Can I expect my dependants to go without basic comforts for the sake of my principles? And corporately: Should my Church own property and negotiate developments and investments? Can and should politics be pacifist? Should I not refuse to pay taxes, especially while Britain pours millions into the nuclear Trident submarine project? And if I refuse to be protected, do I thereby disallow national military defence and dispense with a police force? How should I/we react to international aggression and national crime?

Chastity

Does complete faithfulness within marriage, and total sexual abstinence outside marriage, allow me to find fulfilment and a positive affirmation of my own sexuality? Doesn't it rather tend to cause me to carry guilt if I fall, or become frigidly judgemental of those who do not or cannot measure up to my standards? In my legalistic attitude, do I not offend against love? Can I live a life of purity and emotional freedom and warmth as Jesus and Francis did?

Obedience

Is radical obedience as taught by Jesus and Francis practical in our contemporary world? Are not the possibilities of the first and the thirteenth centuries completely removed from those of the twentieth? If I tried to pattern my obedience on Jesus or Francis, would I not be judged completely mad? And would not this drive people away from the gospel and not welcome them to experience God's love for sinners, in forgiveness and understanding?

I'm not providing answers, but asking questions! Perhaps the world needs such a radical interpretation of the gospel, and perhaps the early Franciscans were among the scandalous few who have lived it out at this level. I end this chapter with some more lines from the *Legend* – enought to jolt us out of our acceptable Christian complacency:

Opinions varied about these men who were so obviously set on following the Gospel: some people declared that they were fools or drunk, but others maintained that such words were not those of folly. One listener said: 'Either these men are following the Lord in great perfection, or they must be demented, since their way of life appears desperate, with little food and going about barefoot and clad in the poorest garments.' For the moment the brothers' manner of holy life frightened those who saw them, and as yet no one was ready to join them. Indeed the young women fled when they saw them approaching from afar for fear of their being madmen.[11]

God of tenderness and mercy:
When I call you Master or Lord, I do not think of you as a tyrant or despot, but as my loving Father who gently receives the vowed obedience of his child;
You call me back from my wayward wandering and set my feet aright; you call me forward into new ways of service and responsibility; you call me inward into unimagined depths of loving communion.
Grant me an unfolding awareness of your purpose and a loving obedience to your will;
For in your will is my peace. Amen.

9 🌺 *Brothers and Sisters*

SAINTS IN LOVE

'A heavenly love can be as real as an earthly love,' says G. K. Chesterton, speaking of the relationship between Francis and

Clare.[1] He helped her to elope into the Franciscan life, defying her parents as he had defied his father. It was like a romantic elopement, for she escaped through the 'coffin door' of her house, fled through the woods, and a procession of torches led her at midnight to the place where she surrendered her life and made her vows.

Clare di Offreduccio was about eighteen years old when Francis accepted her vows and received her on Palm Sunday, 1212. She had known Francis for about two years. Brother Rufino, one of the first friars, was her cousin. From him and the local Assisi gossip she must have heard of Francis' quarrel and break with his father before Bishop Guido in 1206.

During the two years from 1210, Clare was chaperoned by her aunt Bona of Guelficcio, and Francis was accompanied by the prudent brother Philip the Tall. They doubtless talked over the whole journey of conversion, breaking from the world, and the possibility of Clare entering the Franciscan life. It is difficult to know how she envisaged it, but it is thought that Clare was feeling after something of the gospel life of the brothers and not opting for a cloistered, totally enclosed existence. Julien Green surrounds the story with a romantic aura:

When Francis was preaching in the cathedral of San Rufino, he had no idea that a young girl, seventeen years old accompanied by her mother and sister, was listening with passionate attention to the great seducer of souls who spoke of God's love. Francis was not what is called handsome, and he was twelve years older than she. But that didn't matter because, as unsurpassingly beautiful as she was, she welcomed each of his words with an indescribable emotion. He wrenched her out of herself. Together with him she fell in love with Love – and how can you separate Love from love for Love's messenger? Had the two kinds of love interfused? We have only one heart to love God and his creatures. If Clare had been told that she was in love with Francis, she would have been horrified and would not have understood. But after she got home, his voice, at once gentle and vehement, kept following her, preaching penance, scorn for riches, mortification of the flesh.

She could no more resist the impulse to love than he could. It was their nature, hers and his, but this was the first time she had heard him extolling Love, and he revealed to her that their passion was the same: the infinite desire to be one with God.[2]

Anthony Mockler has many radical opinions about the whole Franciscan adventure, and he says plainly:

Clare fell in love with Francis. And Francis, I think committed adultery with her in his heart, and never could forgive himself or womanhood, thereafter ... As for Clare, there is no greater sign of a woman's love for a man than the enthusiasm with which she accepts and follows all his ideals, however extravagant in themselves and however dramatic in their consequences. Clare, I think, loved Francis with all her heart; and for Francis' sake loved all his schemes and all his manoeuvres, even when eventually they excluded her.[3]

But Clare's actions were not those of an adolescent madly flinging herself into an unthought-out situation. She acted carefully, calmly, and after much time and thought.

I find myself moved to inexpressible depths by one who did just what Mockler accuses Clare of doing. I mean Heloise, the lover of Abelard. I cannot but believe that the grace of God is at work in her, despite her protests.

Her letters, burning with the fire of eroticism and desire, reveal a contrasting attitude to Clare's in making her vows. Heloise's love is centred in Abelard, and his castration by his enemies was a sword in her soul. 'You know, beloved,' she writes, 'as the whole world knows, how much I have lost in you, how at one wretched stroke of fortune that supreme act of flagrant treachery robbed me of my very self in robbing me of you.' And she continues:

It was not any sense of vocation which brought me as a young girl to accept the austerities of the cloister, but your bidding alone, and if I deserve no gratitude from you, you may judge for yourself how my labours are in vain. I can expect no reward for this from God, for it is certain that I have done nothing as yet for love of him. When you hurried towards God I followed you, indeed, I went first to take the veil ... I would have no hesitation, God knows, in following you or going ahead at your bidding to the flames of Hell. My heart was not in me but with you, and even now, even more, if it is not with you, it is nowhere; truly, without you, it cannot exist ...

Men call me chaste; they do not know the hypocrite I am. They consider purity of the flesh a virtue, though virtue belongs not to the the body but the soul. I can win praise in the eyes of men but deserve none before God who searches our hearts and loins and sees in our darkness.[4]

Both Clare and Heloise were moved by the grace of God, but how different they were. The measured manner of Clare's decision, her courage and tenacity in the face of family opposition and down through the long years of her vocation reveal a woman in love with God.

But there is no reason why she may not also have been in love with Francis, for the Lord often uses lesser human loves to lead a soul to himself. As Julien Green has it:

Lovers have no psychology because they are out of their heads. Clare was in love with Christ — and, perhaps, with Francis too, but not consciously, because she couldn't make the necessary distinction between them. She was overcome with the joy of surrendering her soul to the man who gave her God; and it is quite possible that, in her extreme euphoria, she fell down at his knees and blurted out her desire to leave the world and its riches to follow Christ.[5]

THE FEMININE ELEMENT

Contemporary writers feel themselves bound to affirm the feminine element in the Franciscan story. It is not enough for them that Francis represents the masculine and Clare the feminine. They need to feel that Francis embraces the feminine *anima* as Clare embraces the masculine *animus*. And perhaps they are right, though we must be careful not to be caught up in the *Zeitgeist* that reads the spirit of our times back into the old story. Take this paragraph from Murray Bodo:

Almost from its very inception the Franciscan life has been infused with both masculine and feminine elements, bringing to the fore the richness of the gospel life or any life when it refuses to be solely masculine or feminine. There is something profoundly womblike about San Damiano and the life that was lived there, as there is something phallic in the brothers' constant forays into the world to preach and witness to the Gospel.[6]

I would like to know how Francis and Clare would have responded to that statement!

Eric Doyle makes a better case when he says that Clare's reception into the Franciscan movement rounded off the story of its origins. Until then, although, as Francis said, the Lord had given him friars, there was something missing from the Order's life. It was the feminine element, which needed to be included explicitly and officially so that the fine balance of the masculine and feminine elements in Francis' own life could be maintained. This is reflected in Francis' tenderness, and the feminine language he used in speaking of the friars' care for one another. Take the first paragraph in his instructions for *Religious Life in Hermitages*:

> Not more than three or at most four friars should go together to a hermitage to lead a religious life there. Two of these should act as mothers, with the other two, or the other one, as their children. The mothers are to lead the life of Martha; the other two, the life of Mary Magdalen.[7]

It may be that Clare really wanted to be a fraternal member of the First Order, and not a cloistered foundress of the Second Order. We have little information about Clare's religious life for the first three years. Presumably she and her four companions followed the Rule which Pope Innocent III had approved for Francis in 1209. Although their life was not canonically cloistered, we catch a glimpse of certain enclosure in the first days at San Damiano from Celano:

> After a few days, she moved to the church of San Angelo di Panzo. But as her soul was not fully at rest there, at the advice of the Blessed Francis she removed at last to the church of San Damiano ... In the prison of this little cloister Clare shut herself up for the love of her heavenly spouse. Here she hid herself from the turmoil of the world and imprisoned her body as long as she lived.[8]

Francis did not receive Clare under sufferance. He welcomed her with open arms, and himself conferred the rough habit and cut off her beautiful hair. Bishop Guido was in on the secret, but Francis took charge of her reception, and by that very act integrated the feminine with the masculine in the Franciscan life. This fact has to be set against his apprehensions about women.

In his *A New Fioretti*, John Moorman reproduces the story in which Francis exclaims: 'God has taken away our wives, and now the devil has given us sisters.' But that may well be put into the mouth of Clare when confronted with a certain kind of friar: 'God has taken away our husbands, and now the devil has given us brothers.' The real relationship between them is revealed in words which Clare wrote shortly before her death:

> When this blessed Father was assured that nothing could persuade us to turn back, neither poverty, nor labour, nor tribulations, but that on the contrary all was becoming for us an ineffable delight, he sent us the following letter dictated by his paternal affection: 'Since you are become the daughters and servants of a heavenly Father and the spouses of the Holy Spirit, in choosing to live according to the perfection of the Gospel, I promise you always to watch over you as over my friars themselves.'[9]

In his life of Francis, Lord Longford says that though the old maxim enjoins a monk always to fly from women and bishops, Francis did neither. He found celibacy difficult anyway, and Clare radiated light and warmth as he did, and between them there was an unusually tender relationship. Legend speaks of the almost mystical bond of the sublime love they shared, 'free from all animal urges, but not free from a genuine man/woman relationship'.

> This man-to-woman love of Francis for Clare is not accepted by a number of his many biographers, but there is no gainsaying the fact that his love for her was profound. He turned to her continually for understanding and sympathy as to no one else. He, her superior, counsellor, and friend, was also her child. Her courage and steadfastness were there to offer him comfort and to renew his strength. Her unswerving devotion to him could be held to justify all assumptions.[10]

Longford also recalls the legend of the wicked innkeeper and the roses. Francis and Clare were walking to Spello one winter's day in 1215, before the Order was enclosed, to see the Camaldolese nuns who had asked for the Franciscan Rule. They went into an inn where the 'evil-minded innkeeper' grumbled that it was scandalous for them to be tramping the country together under cover of religion. It was a Friday, and he placed a fat fowl on the table to put them in the wrong. Francis made the sign of the cross over the fowl, which immediately was transformed into a fish, to the consternation of the innkeeper!

When they left Spello, Francis bade Clare return by the upper path while he took the valley road. Clare had not heard the inn-keeper's remark, and was at a loss to understand, yet she made to obey Francis, asking him when they would meet again. 'When the roses bloom on Mount Subasio,' he replied.

Clare went on ahead, puzzled by his behaviour, but as she walked the snow melted before her and briar roses bloomed on the juniper bushes around her. She gathered them in her arms, ran down the hill to Francis — so together they walked back to Assisi![11]

BROTHERS AND SISTERS

We have seen that when Francis began responding to the divine call God gave him brothers. That's where he began. And when Clare responded, God gave her sisters.

Clare had two familial sisters, Agnes and Beatrice — both of whom joined her. She had always been close to Agnes, but when Clare left home 'a marvellous love took hold of them both'. She prayed that the affinity of spirit which they had always felt might become a unity of will in the service of God. So it was with joy that Clare received Agnes at San Damiano, where she lived for some years. When Agnes was sent to establish the Poor Clare house in Florence, she felt her separation deeply, and wrote: 'I suffer great distress and immense sadness because I have been physically separated from you and my other sisters with whom I had hoped to live and die.'[12] She did later return to San Damiano, and was present at Clare's deathbed.

A present-day Poor Clare writes movingly of the common love between Francis and Clare, and between Clare, Agnes, and her sisters, in which discipline is a basic element. Neither Clare nor Agnes had shrunk from their separation, because they both loved in Christ, and their common love was in that context:

> If Agnes could write so vehemently from Florence, one wonders how she had reacted when the idea of going there had first been mooted, but obviously Clare had not shrunk from it on that score, nor had she softened the edges in any way. This was not because she was hard but because she understood that the first person to whom we are sister and brother is Christ himself. Whatever the physical relationship, it is in Christ that we find our primary relationship, and so the work of Christ, which is

the work of the Father, must be top priority in all situations. This is why Francis used to call Clare Christiana, the Christian, because he saw her as a true sister of Christ, our brother.[13]

In the next generation, we find Bonaventure writing a *Letter to a Poor Clare* in which there is mutual warmth and openness, and which place the goal and end of our genuine human love in the context of the sacred humanity of Jesus, and this leads to mystical union with the divine Christ:

> Draw near, dear handmaiden, with loving feet to Jesus wounded, to Jesus crowned with thorns, to Jesus fastened to the gibbet of the cross; and be not content, as the blessed apostle Thomas was, merely to see in his hands the print of the nails or to thrust your hand into his side; but rather go right in, through the opening in his side, to the very heart of Jesus where, transformed by most burning love for Christ, held by the nails of divine love, pierced by the lance of profound charity and wounded by the sword of deep compassion, you will know no other wish or desire or hope or consolation except to die with Christ upon the cross ...[14]

In the same generation, we find one of the great Franciscan tertiaries and mystics, Angela of Foligno, who, after nominal membership in the Third Order, was visited by a remarkable vision on the way to the shrine of St Francis. This began a series of mystical visions and experiences which she related to her astonished cousin Brother Arnaldo of the Friars Minor, who recorded them at her dictation. Here again is displayed a mutual warmth and affection within the love of God. Her relation with Arnaldo brought her into close touch with the friars, and she certainly lived and prayed in the atmosphere of the poetry of Jacopone da Todi.

This early Franciscan pattern is one which should nourish our relationships today. There is a great deal of gender conflict in the world and in the Church. It would be a great loss to ourselves and to the Franciscan witness if mutual love and tenderness were not seen to be present in our lives. If men, women, and children are not able to love one another within the family of Jesus and Francis, then let us stop telling other people what they should be thinking and doing.

I want to close this chapter with one of my favourite Francis-Clare stories. Francis was burdened and worried about how Clare was faring. He and Leo were passing a fresh-water fountain that bubbled into a clear trough. Francis gazed long and deeply into the water, then lifted his head and looked at Leo. 'Brother Leo, little lamb of God, what do you think I have seen in the water of this fountain?' he asked. 'The moon, father,' replied Leo somewhat drily. 'No, Brother Leo, it is not the moon that I have seen in the water, but by the merciful grace of God I have seen the face of our Sister Clare, so pure and radiant with holy joy, that all my misgivings are vanished.'[15]

As Sister Francis Teresa says of them: 'They were brother and sister to everything and everyone, and as they lived this out in daily life, Clare and Francis worshipped the God who is Father and Mother of all that is.'[16]

Lord of all life and love:
In your servants Francis and Clare you mingled his kinship with
  all creation and her clear light of compassion;
Stir up in us a new sense of wonder in all human relationships,
  and let all our human loves be seen in the greater Calvary
  love of your dear Son, our Saviour Jesus. Amen.

10 ❧ *Missionary Fervour*

Pope Innocent III died in Perugia in 1216. Francis was there. So
was Jacques de Vitry, bishop-elect of Acre, who wrote the story
of how Innocent's courtiers abandoned him in his dying hours.

The body of the great medieval pope was carried in its open coffin to the cathedral for the next day's funeral. 'It was on that day that I really understood the nothingness of grandeur here below,' says Jacques de Vitry. 'The night preceding the funeral, robbers broke in and despoiled the pope of everything precious upon him. I saw with my own eyes his body, half naked, lying in the midst of the church, already stinking.'

He goes on, in a letter, to bewail the state of the Church and the worldliness of the curia and clergy, and their lack of spirituality and zeal for God. Then he makes an exception and writes glowingly of Francis and the friars:

> What I saw which was consoling was the large number of men and women who had renounced their wealth, had quitted the world for love of Christ. These men who bore the name of Friars Minor are held by the Pope and the Cardinals in the highest esteem. Disinteresting themselves absolutely in temporal things they consecrate all their efforts to withdraw from the world souls in peril and to induce them to follow them. Thanks be to God, they have already had important success and made numerous conquests, for they are adepts in recruiting others and their hearers multiply of themselves. As for their manner of life, it is that of the Primitive Church where, as the Scripture says, the multitude of believers had but one heart and one soul. By day they are found in the towns and villages preaching, or at work; at night they return to their hermitages where they give themselves in solitude to prayer.

He also comments on the warm fellowship of their annual Chapters, and the sheer joy which spread around the Italian Peninsula 'over Lombardy, in Tuscany and even as far as Apulia and Sicily'. Four years later, speaking of their poverty and simplicity, he says: 'This Religion is multiplied through the whole world.'[1]

Evangelism flows from evangelical conversion, and such was the treasure of love, joy, and peace that was part of the Franciscan experience, it had to be shared. It was a matter of the zealous overflow of the quality of life and fellowship, the fire of which was kindled in Umbria, and soon spread to the ends of the earth.

ZEAL NOT ENOUGH

But there were problems. Scripture warns against a zeal without proper enlightenment, and the kind of fervent and provocative proclamation which leads to fanaticism.[2] There was always the danger that an enthusiastic elite like the early friars, set ablaze by enthusiasm for the gospel, could rush around the world, ill-prepared and emotionally charged.

The nature of the Franciscan experience has always been open to emotionalism. This certainly led to fanaticism among the *zelanti*, the Spiritual friars who became the later Observants, in contrast to the *mitigati* friars who became known as the Conventuals.

A Missionary Chapter took place in 1217, following the death of Pope Innocent III. There was a spirit of risk and adventure abroad, and Francis challenged the friars, saying that he would not send the brothers to face privation and persecution that he would not himself be prepared to undergo. There was also the glory of martyrdom, which Francis, and many of the friars, both invited and welcomed.

They were neither called nor expected in the countries to which they would go; they had no knowledge of the languages, cultures, or traditions of those regions; and they would go without money, authorization, or ecclesial recommendation. It was really a mad escapade — but they were fools for Christ!

In the midst of all this, Francis gave them advice in which he speaks some of the most inspired words, containing Franciscan spirituality in a nutshell:

> Take the road two and two in the Name of the Lord. Be humble and sincere. Keep silence from dawn until after Terce, praying to God in your hearts, and do not indulge in idle and unprofitable conversation. Although you are travelling, let your words be as humble and devout as in a hermitage or cell. For wherever we are, or wherever we go, we always take our cell with us; for Brother Body is our cell, and our soul is the hermit who lives in it, constantly praying to God and meditating on Him. If the soul cannot remain quiet in its cell, then a cell made with hands is of little value to a Religious.[3]

It was Francis' intention to go to France because of his love for things French, so he went off to the shrine of St Peter and St Paul in Rome to pray for the enterprise. But in Florence he met Cardinal Hugolino, who persuaded him that he was needed in Italy, both for the consolidation of the Order and because he knew of the insufficient preparation and the opposition to the friars because of their ignorance.

Francis protested that it would be shameful to send his brothers off to face dangers and persecutions while he remained in safety at home. Hugolino replied that he was precipitate in sending the brothers, and that the work of consolidation was primary. Francis retorted: 'My Lord, God wills that my friars shall spread over the whole world, and not only in Christian lands where they are welcome, but even among the infidels who will receive them and be converted by their words.'[4]

It was in 1262 that Brother Jordan di Giano related the missionary story of those early days. He honestly describes the failures of various missions and his own predicament of being caught up in a voluntary group to go to the dreaded Germany. 'There are two things which I daily asked of God,' he writes. 'Firstly, not to fall into the Cathar's heresy; secondly, not to be the victim of German ferocity.'

After telling the story of persecution, cruelty, beating, and nakedness in Hungary, and confessing the abandonment of the mission, he goes on to describe the impossibility of the first German mission.

John of Penna led sixty friars, none of whom knew more than the German word *Ja*. When they were asked if they were hungry, it served them well; but when they were asked if they were the Lombard heretics, it landed them naked in the pillory, flogged and bleeding. Jordan sums up the failure of the missions of 1217 by saying, with Ecclesiastes, that there is a time for everything under the sun, and that this was not it![5]

In 1220, the learned and able German Caesar of Speyer joined the Order. He had studied in Paris and was a convert of Brother Elias. So in 1221, at the Pentecost Chapter, he was invited to lead a new mission to Germany.

Francis indicated that he wanted friars to volunteer, and Jordan, who tells the story, reminds us of the savage ferocity of the Germans and that only those who looked for martyrdom should dare go. However, ninety brothers offered, some of them Germans, and among them John of Piancarpino, who would later become one of the great Franciscan missionaries to China and Mongolia.

Jordan's account is amusing, for he regretted not having known the friars who had previously been martyred in Morocco, so he went to talk with the courageous ninety who were willing to journey to Germany. The lively and jocular Palmerius took hold of Jordan and said: 'You, too, are coming with us.' 'No, no,' Jordan answered quickly, 'I am only come to make your acquaintance.' But the friars would not let him go.

When Caesar approached the group, they drew attention to Jordan, but he again protested. 'Not at all, never have I wished to go to Germany; besides it is a cold country which is very bad for my health.'

The crunch came when Brother Elias ordered Jordan under obedience to come to a decision to say yes or no. He was perplexed because he didn't want to refuse and look like a coward, and yet he knew that he might well deny his faith under torture, and he had no ambition to be a martyr.

All this is refreshingly honest. Jordan went off to a friar who had lost his breeches fifteen times to the taunting persecutors in Hungary, and asked his advice. He was told to express no preference to Brother Elias, but to leave it to him. 'And that is how I was amongst those who planted the Order in Germany,' he concludes.

Jordan's fears were not fulfilled. They were well prepared this time, communicating Franciscan joy, spontaneity, and discipline, making friends of the common people, counting numerous converts, and planting friaries throughout Germany and then into Bohemia, Poland, Romania, and Norway.[6]

WELCOME AND GROWTH IN BRITAIN

We are fortunate in having *The Chronicle of Thomas of Eccleston*, describing the beginnings of the English Province, with its simplicity, poverty, and fervour. It was initiated by the 1223 Chapter, when ten friars under the Blessed Agnello of Pisa set out for Dover, arriving in September 1224.

Their passage was paid by the Benedictines of Fécamp, and from Dover they divided. Five remained at Canterbury, and the other four went to London. A house was later established at Oxford, and some scholarly students and masters joined them.

Some of these scholarly friars in Oxford acted as labourers, carrying stones and mortar to build a convent, as Francis had laboured in the churches around Assisi. Others who followed university courses had to wade barefoot and up to their knees through swampy marshland to get to their lectures.

In Canterbury, the chapel was built in a single day, but at first they had use of only a single schoolroom in the evenings, where they were filled with joy as they warmed themselves around what was left of the fire and heated up the dregs of beer from the boys' left-overs.

In 1225, they established houses in Northampton, Norwich, and Cambridge, where they shared a house with the prisoners of the city.

Thomas illustrates the stature and simplicity of the first friars in England by telling the story of Brother Salomon, who during the winter was so cold and ill that the friars thought he would die. They had no wood for a fire, so they decided that they would do what pigs did in like extremity. The lay around and snuggled up to him, so warming and reviving him.

There were added to these friars names like Adam Marsh, Richard of Cornwall, Robert Grosseteste, master at Oxford and Bishop of Lincoln, and Roger Bacon, philosopher, theologian, and scientist.

Albert of Pisa said of these early friars that three things distinguished them — their bare feet, their coarse clothing, and their refusal to touch any money. This would have cheered Francis, and when holy John of Parma visited them in 1248 he cried: 'Would that a province such as this had been set in the midst of the world that it might be an example to all.'

Scottish, Irish, and Welsh convents soon sprang up, but there were various disagreements about authority, independence, and ecclesiastical politics. By about 1255 there were over fifty friaries and more than 1,200 friars in the British Isles. The poverty and simplicity of the early days gave way to specially constructed houses, as Bonaventure advised, and the land produced gardens and vegetables.

Many of the friars saw this as simple common sense, but there are stories such as that of Stephen of Belase, the *custos* of Hereford, who was so grieved by the increasing laxity that he publicly burst into tears. Nevertheless, the English friars were known for some time as the Brothers of the Order of the Apostles because their life recalled the humility of the disciples of Christ.

CRUSADING CONQUEST OR EVANGELISM

The Church at the beginning of the thirteenth century felt the need to combat heresy and somehow convert or silence heretics — often using worldly wisdom and carnal, violent means. The crusading spirit was also alive in the desire to stem the flood-tide of Islam and gain possession of the holy places of Palestine. But it was hardly aware of the positive sharing of compassion and joy that was the evangelistic vision of Francis.

Christendom was troubled first by the might and zeal of Islam to the east, west, and south, and then by the even greater danger of the appearance of the Mongols of Asia under the charismatic Genghis Khan.

Francis' vision was not that of controlling heretics, infidels, or heathen to make Europe or the world safe for Christianity. It was the sharing of the treasure of the gospel, the overflow of peace, joy, and compassion in a universal fraternity that was inclusive of humanity and creation.

In 1220, he returned from his expedition to Egypt (of which more later), his mind and heart full of sorrow over the moral and spiritual bankruptcy of the crusade mentality, but with a vision of the need for Christ among Christians and Saracens. So there appears in the Rule of 1221 the following:

> The friars who are inspired by God to work as missionaries among the Saracens and other unbelievers must get permission to go from their minister, who is their servant. The minister, for his part, should give them permission and raise no objection, if he sees that they are suitable ... No matter where they are, the friars must always remember that they have given themselves up completely and handed over their whole selves to our Lord Jesus Christ, and so they should be prepared to expose themselves to every enemy, visible or invisible, for love of him.[7]

This encouraging commission is surrounded by gospel tests about self-sacrifice for the love of Christ, and provides a powerful evangelistic motivation full of compassion and peace.

So the story of the early Franciscan missions to the Holy Land, Islamic Europe, North Africa, and Asia is a powerful, energetic, adventurous, and romantic one.[8] There are three Franciscans who incarnate the Franciscan vision with zeal, courage, and charisma. One is Ramon Lull, of the Third Order, whose amazing life and missionary zeal shine in the annals of the tertiaries.[9] The other two are John of Piancarpino and John of Montecorvino, who journeyed into the Tartar territories of Mongolia.

Christendom and Islam had a common enemy in the Mongol Empire of the East. In 1206, Genghis Khan set out with a vision of world conquest. He soon conquered Peking in the East, with

Tartar armies in India, Afghanistan, Georgia, the Caucasus, and south Russia. By about 1540 they swept across Russia, marching into Kiev, Poland, and Hungary, some even reaching Dalmatia.

Pope Innocent IV sent an embassy to the invaders in the person of the Franciscan friar John of Piancarpino, a corpulent but holy and zealous friar, with his companion Benedict the Pole.

They spent the winter of 1245–6 in Poland, and with the thaw they turned east, 'not knowing whether they were going to death or life'. Soon into the Tartar outposts, they were passed on from one to another until it was decided to send them to the Great Khan. So they were forced to ride over 3,000 miles through the Great Steppes at a deadly pace, which would have been an ordeal for the toughest of horsemen, but for an elderly friar who was extremely fat and in poor health, was one of the most remarkable physical feats of endurance on record.

In July 1246, they reached Karakoram in Outer Mongolia for the enthronement of the Great Khan Guyuk, grandson of Genghis. The Franciscans were welcomed among the Mongol chieftains, remaining until November, when they were given a letter from Guyuk to the pope. Their return journey in the depths of winter was even more heroic than the outward journey.

The letter was a menacing one, warning Christendom of dire things to come. But Christopher Dawson, in *The Mongol Mission*, tells the amazing story of Franciscan fervour during the next few years, with Franciscans like William of Rebruk blazing a trail into Mongolia. There were meetings with Nestorian Christians and a sprinkling of Western Christians who had previously been taken prisoner. We have a moving picture of William, in a worn habit, standing before the powerful Mangu Khan, as he describes the scene: 'He stretched out toward me the staff on which he was leaning, saying, "Fear not." I smiled and said quietly, "If I were afraid I would not have come here."'

John of Montecorvino was chosen by Pope Nicholas IV as a missionary to China in 1291. He was welcomed by the emporer Timor at Cambalech (Peking), the capital of the Mongol Empire. He built a church and a convent, and, with an eye to a future community and priesthood, he purchased boys to be baptized and trained. In a letter dated 1305, he says he had baptized about 6,000 people, and continues:

Also I have purchased by degrees forty boys [of the] sons of the pagans, between seven and eleven years old, who as yet knew no religion. Here I baptized them and taught them Latin and our rite, and I wrote for them about thirty psalters and hymnaries and two breviaries by which eleven boys now know the office. And they keep choir and say the offices as in a convent whether I am there or not. And several of them write psalters and other suitable things. And the Lord Emperor takes much delight in their singing. And I ring the bells for all the Hours and sing the divine office with my choir of 'babes and sucklings'. But we sing by heart because we have no books with notes.[10]

The mission flourished by evangelism, translation of the New Testament and Psalms, liturgical instruction, and catechism. John was consequently joined by three Franciscan bishops and consecrated Archbishop of Cambalech. He spent thirty-five years expending his evangelistic and pastoral energy in the mission, and saw it grow in numbers and quality. He died there in the winter of 1328–9, at eighty-one years of age. John Moorman evaluates the worth of such Franciscan leaders:

With men like Piancarpino and Montecorvino as its leaders the story of the Franciscan mission to the East in the first century or so after the death of S. Francis is a story of great enterprise and great devotion. It demanded of those who took part in it high qualities of courage and endurance, for the dangers were many and the tax on a man's physical and moral strength was heavy. Perhaps only friars could have undertaken such work, for they were inspired and fortified by a great love of souls, and had learned to travel light while about their Master's business. Francis had taught his friars to be reckless; and those who set out to visit the Tartars or to cross the Gobi desert could take little thought for the morrow.[11]

This chapter on missionary fervour is not out of place in our understanding of Franciscan spirituality, for we are invited to drink from the same source as did the missionary heroes we have been considering. We may not be called to struggle through the blizzards of the Steppes and the dark valleys of Outer Mongolia in search of souls for Christ, but we need the same fervour and anointing for the task to which God has called us. Yet having written that last sentence, I have before me a letter from a young

Christian writing from Inner Mongolia, doing medical VSO work there, enquiring about the possibility of a Franciscan vocation.

A FRANCISCAN PERSPECTIVE ON MISSION

Christendom has often misrepresented the way of Christ. The radical nature of Jesus' life and ministry interpreted and lived by St Francis is not compatible with the laxity of any establishment.

As soon as the early Church came under the moulding hand of the Constantinian regime, there emerged a mixture of religion and politics that served the state. Christian society was on the way to becoming synonymous with pagan power, and this produced the reaction of the Desert Fathers (and Mothers), who would not be dictated to by a decadent state, nor influenced by the values and policies of a state ruled by ambition, power, and violence.

Medieval times saw the triumph of worldliness in the Church, in the conflict and warfare between pope and emperor. Pope Innocent III is the great illustration of this, and it is ironic that it was this pope whose decaying body was stripped and desecrated in the cathedral at Perugia the night before his funeral, causing Brother Mansuetus to comment: 'No beggar died such a miserable and wretched death as a pope.'

This is the Church which persecuted heretics to torture and death, massacred Jews and Muslims in crusades, and forcibly converted nations and people under pain of death. Because of a departure from Francis' vision, we even find some later friars caught up in the darker areas of the Inquisition.

In such a period, God raised up Francis to rebuild the tottering Church, and the dark background makes Francis' venture among the Muslims in 1219 all the more enlightening.

At Damietta he found the crusading army filled with licence and immorality, and buoyed up with ambitions of pillage and lust. He learned that a decisive attack was to be launched upon the Saracens, and, turning to Brother Illuminato, told him that the Lord had revealed to him that they would be miserably defeated.

'Ought I to warn them?' questioned Francis. 'If I speak, they will take me for a madman; if I keep silent my conscience will reproach me. How does it appear to you, my brother?'

'The judgment of men is nothing,' came the reply. 'After all this is not the first time you have been taken for a madman. Free your conscience and tell them the truth for the love of God.'

His word was rejected, and there was a disaster. Six thousand men were slain, and Francis wept over the violence of religious men and the lust and avarice of the victors.[12]

Over a period, Francis ministered to the crusader army and went into the enemy camp to preach Christ, though he must have been torn in half to face the contradictions of such military might crusading in the name of the Prince of Peace.

When Francis and Illuminato approached the Sultan's men, they were comforted by the sight of two sheep browsing, for it reminded them that they were like sheep among wolves. Soon they were taken and beaten by the Saracens, until Francis shouted: 'Soldan, Soldan!' and then they were led, chained, to Melek-el-Kamel.

Bonaventure tells the story of Francis preaching and of the Sultan's willingness to listen and debate. Then Francis threw down a challenge:

> If you are willing to become converts to Christ, you and your people, I shall be only too glad to stay with you for love of him. But if you are afraid to abandon the law of Mahomet for Christ's sake, then light a big fire and I will go into it with your priests. That will show you which faith is more sure and more holy.[13]

The Sultan caught sight of one of his leading priests slipping away at Francis' words, and said that his priests would not accept such a challenge, nor would he convert, for it would cause a revolt among his people.

He vainly offered money and gifts, but Francis turned sadly away, realizing that the Sultan would not turn to Christ, nor would he send Francis to martyrdom. Both friars were given safe passage back to the Christian camp, perhaps realizing the immense difficulties of preaching Christ from a context of violence and bloodshed.

MISSIONARY ZEAL AND FERVOUR TODAY

We have come a long way from medieval times, but nearly eight hundred years later Europe is torn by religious intolerance and persecution, with adherents of major religions at one another's throats.

There is another way — the way of Jesus and the vision of Francis, where faith is shared but not imposed, and where people of different faiths meet for genuine dialogue and reciprocated service and compassion.

The Franciscan pattern in the wider Church is one in which both the evangelical and the catholic nature of the gospel is treasured, and both these traditions hold to the uniqueness of Christ as universal Saviour. In Jesus, the eternal Word has become incarnate, and he cannot be placed in a pantheon among other gods.

The danger in such an affirmation, among certain groups, is an exclusivism which sees evangelism only in terms of imposing one's own views without dialogue, understanding, or sharing. Dialogue means not only sharing the revealed Christ with those of other faiths and none, but also discovering the hidden Christ among them. It implies an open ear and heart, learning the positive truths that are among the treasures of other faith traditions, and making genuine friends with Buddhists, Hindus, Sufis, and others. I think now of the gracious group of Sikhs with whom we shared visits at Glasshampton and exchanged gifts. And I'm told that such reciprocal visits continue.

Franciscan experience is not only believing in the historical Jesus who lived, loved, died, and rose for us, but in the eternal Christ, the second Person of the Holy Trinity, who dwelt in the bosom of the Father from all eternity and is the true Light who enlightens *everyone* coming into the world.

This means that the light of Christ can be found in men, women, and children around the world whose hearts are turned towards love and truth. Our mission, then, is to share the gospel of the forgiving love of God in Christ with them, and to discover the hidden Christ within their traditions.

Evangelical fervour and zeal will then be treasured, but dogmatic exclusivism which engenders fanaticism will be avoided. This is a delicate middle path, with the dangers of *syncretism* on the one hand, and *fundamentalism* on the other. The light of Francis, under the Holy Spirit, will enable us to maintain a joyful middle way that does not compromise a full-blooded affirmation of the gospel.

Lord Jesus Christ:
Our brother Francis of Assisi was filled with the love and
*   zeal of your holy gospel;*
He carried its message into the heart of violent religious
*   fanaticisms in simple trust, faith, and peace.*
Grant us that same spirit of universal wisdom, tolerance, and

97

understanding, that we may share the treasures of your gospel with those of other faiths, and learn in their friendship the hiddenness of your Holy Spirit of truth.
To the praise of your dear Name. Amen.

11 ❧ The Third Order

THIRD ORDER BEGINNINGS

From what we have already seen, it is clear that the magnetic and charismatic enthusiasm of Francis was infectious, causing men and women to leave their families, relinquish their possessions, and follow Christ literally, under the banner of Francis in the First Order of Friars or the Second Order of Poor Clares.

When faced with such men and women, Francis had no doubt about challenging them with the gospel call, for the riches of the Kingdom of God were worth more than all the treasures of the world. For such a pearl of great price these converts surrendered all the worldly baubles that appeared worthless when compared with the gospel pearl that Francis held up for all to see. He gathered these people joyfully into the company of the friars or the St Damiano sisters, and they lived by the simple rule of the gospel that Pope Innocent III had approved at the beginning of the adventure in 1209.

But there was one group which caused Francis some perplexity at first. He would enter into some village or market-square and begin to preach. Crowds would gather and be caught up in the glory and wonder of a living faith that transformed the *Poverello* and caught up the common people under the influence of the Holy Spirit. 'Men ran, and women too ran, clerics hurried, and religious hastened that they might see and hear the holy man of God who seemed to all to be a man of another world.'[1]

The *Fioretti* illustrates such a happening in the village of Cannara in 1212, where the fervour of Francis' preaching caused such a holy uproar that practically the whole village wanted to abandon their home, and follow him.

He realized that if he went on like this whole boroughs would be depopulated, ordinary life would be disrupted, and family and commerical relations would have no base. The *Fioretti* reveals this wisdom when he said: '"Don't be in a hurry and don't leave, for I will arrange what you should do for the salvation of your souls." And from that time he planned to organize the Third Order ... for the salvation of all people everywhere.'[2]

Celano portrays the great company of people under the threefold Franciscan banner:

Many put aside worldly cares and gained knowledge of themselves from the life and teaching of the most blessed Francis, and they longed to attain love and reverence for their Creator. Many of the people, both noble and ignoble, cleric and lay, impelled by divine inspiration, began to come to St Francis, wanting to carry on the battle constantly under his discipline and leadership ... and according to his plan the Church is being renewed in both sexes, and the threefold army [*trina militia*] ... is triumphing. To all he gave a norm of life, and he showed in truth the way of salvation to every walk of life.[3]

THE WORLDWIDE FAMILY OF FRANCIS

There were a number of years during which the increasing numbers of people who wanted to follow Christ in the light of Francis measured their lives under the influence of the friars and sisters with no rule but the gospel and the spiritual kinship of family likeness that bound them together.

Some of them actually surrendered everything and explored the hermit life of prayer, but most of them had children to provide for, work they could not abandon, and other commitments that they felt God had called them to complete.

We have mentioned Count Orlando, who, in 1213, gifted Mount La Verna to Francis and divided his time and talents between his responsibilities and the needs of the friars.

The Lady Giocoma was another who could not simply part with the feudal possessions of family (not personal) estates. But the spirit of poverty pervaded all her attitudes, and in 1217 she made a deed renouncing family claims to property that was in legal dispute. This also manifested the tertiary practice of avoiding litigation.[4]

It was not until 1221 that Francis and Cardinal Hugolino together composed a Rule for the Third Order. But it is commonly thought that Francis' own *Letter to All Christians*, which he wrote about 1214, served as a basis for the emerging tertiaries. It expressed Francis' mind and heart, couched in his inimitable style of gospel joy and enthusiasm. The later 1221 *Rule of the Third Order* is heavily influenced by an ecclesiastical mind and legalistic language, but the *Letter* is an overflow of the gospel and of the Acts of the Apostles in its apostolic fervour and literal following of Jesus: 'To all Christians, religious, clerics and layfolk, men and women; to everyone in the whole world, Brother Francis, their servant and subject, sends his humble respects, imploring for them true peace from heaven and sincere love in God.'[5]

It must be read and savoured as an intimate letter from Francis' heart, in which the life of the disciple is grounded firmly in the doctrine of Jesus, a life of grace initiated and empowered by the Holy Spirit. If believers live in the Spirit, they become the spouse of Jesus, mystically united to his divine life; they become the brothers and sisters of the elder Brother Jesus in doing the Father's will; they become the mother of Jesus in bearing him in the inmost soul, allowing his love to radiate from their hearts and bodies.

King David had his three heroic men, his thirty faithful warriors, and his wider army. Jesus had the three who were close to his heart, the faithful band of disciples, and the wider circle of seventy-two.[6] Francis, in turn, had those special ones 'who were with him', then the original eleven who went with him to Rome in 1209, and the Three Orders, who all together join in an equal apostolic dance of love and joy down to the present day.

For some years, the Third Order did not constitute a separate organization, but were secular penitents. It was probably during Francis' mission to the East that Cardinal Hugolino saw the need of a Rule and organization distinct from the friars.

The two vicars Francis had left in charge when he went to the Holy Land in 1219 foisted a more monastic regime on to the friars. The emerging *Conventual* party opposed a formal dependence of the penitents and later Third Order, whereas the *Spiritual* party always favoured a close relationship. Cuthbert thinks that this caused some of the penitents to draw themselves together in some sort of defensive league to affirm their following of Francis and to claim direction by the friars.[7]

This may have pushed Hugolino to put his scheme forward, but he also had clear precedent in his legatine journeys in Lombardy, where he had met up with the Humiliati fraternity of lay penitents. Pope Innocent III had approved a rule for them in 1201.[8]

So when Francis returned from the East, he and Cardinal Hugolino met during the winter of 1220–1 and composed a Third Order Rule. The original is lost, and the earliest version known to us is the *Capestrano Rule* dating from 1228. As we have said, it lacks the evangelical fervour and idealism of early Franciscanism, being mainly concerned with regulations for external conduct, plus moral and religious counsel. But behind this Rule, whether its inspirational sections are lost or not, lies the whole life, teaching, and experience of the charismatic Francis, a man aflame with the love of God, radiant with the joy of Christ, imbued with the dynamic power of the Holy Spirit – the model for all Three Orders.

With its emergence as a distinct organization, the Third Order was subject to the ecclesiastical and not the secular courts. The magistrates of the commune now had no right to enforce oaths, bearing of arms, or civic office upon its members. They therefore became a social force to be reckoned with — a body of citizens protected by the law of the Church. Pope Honorius III actually intervened on behalf of the penitents of Faenza in December 1221, ordering the Bishop of Rimini to protect them against the magistrates.[9]

Francis did not envisage political action or disobedience. He simply enjoined gospel principles on disciples of peace and justice. But the implications of gospel obedience soon became evident in a refusal of the Third Order Penitents to take oaths commanding obedience to secular calls to feuds and wars. Neither would they participate in public offices involving corruption and party political favour, nor subscribe to the system of usury and dishonesty which pervaded contemporary commercial enterprise in the emerging market economy of the communes and merchants.

There are a number of papal bulls from 1227–34 that indicate the excitement of spiritual discipleship, and the furore within the secular empire as a result of Third Order Franciscan spirituality.[10] It was not that Francis sought political influence. He was a gospel-man, and everything else flowed from that. P. H. Felder makes the point succinctly:

> That St Francis was a social reformer such as, since Jesus Christ, the world had not seen, is generally admitted today. There is no doubt much truth in this and other similar views, but it should be said that neither in his writings nor in his discourse was St Francis preoccupied with social and political needs. Like Christ he seemed indifferent to the temporal fate of parties and groups. It was the individual alone and his eternal salvation that counted in his eyes. Certainly he preached the love of one's neighbour, peace, interior happiness, the right of each to accomplish his supernatural destiny. But that is the Gospel, the practice of which, as we know, is entirely favourable to the temporal happiness both of individuals and of societies. It would be better then to say that the political and social rôle of the Poverello was to give the Gospel to souls.[11]

So, from 1221, wherever the Friars Minor and the Poor Clares were established, the Third Order also appeared. It spread itself over the whole world, and the Church raised its members by the hundreds to canonized sainthood. Kings like St Louis of France and St Ferdinand of Castile are among them; Princesses like St Elizabeth of Hungary; former sinners like Margaret of Cortona and Angela of Foligno; innocent children like St Rose of Viterbo; and priests like the Curé d'Ars, and numerous popes. Reckoned among them also are illustrious people like Dante, Petrarch, Raphael, Michelangelo, Giotti, Murillo, Galvani, Volta, Columbus, Palestrina, and Liszt, apart from the 255 Blessed of all conditions inscribed in the Franciscan martyrology.

It is not my intention to pursue a history of the Third Order.[12] Suffice it to say that various editions of the Rule were in use in different parts of the world. So in 1289 some Italian tertiaries appealed to Pope Nicholas IV to issue an authoritative version, which he did in the Bull *Supra montem*, containing the definitive Rule which has been in use ever since.

As to increasing numbers, in 1451 John of Capistrano estimated that there were 600,000 Tertiaries in Italy alone, and by 1447 the Bull of Pope Nicholas V, *Pastoralis officii*, constituted a Third Order Regular for those communal tertiaries who did not join the First or Second Order, yet wanted a more monastic and conventual life, with their own officers, provinces, chapters, statutes, solemn vows, and distinctive habit. These became completely separate from the secular tertiaries, who continued and multiplied as before.

THE THIRD ORDER TODAY

This book is not written to gain converts or adherents to an organized form of the Franciscan life, whether Roman or Anglican, for it is clear that Francis has many followers who have no desire or need for a formal attachment. It is enough for them that there is someone like Francis who is ablaze with love for God and compassion for all, to whom they can look as an elder brother under Christ.

But it is nevertheless a fact that there are many thousands of people throughout the world who live today as members of the Third Order of St Francis in the Roman Catholic communion, and a lesser number who belong to the Third Order of The Society of St Francis in the Anglican communion.

There are also Lutheran and other Franciscan groups within the Church, but as I am a friar of the Anglican First Order (SSF), I shall say a few things about our own Third Order.

A Christian does not necessarily believe more sincerely or function more fervently by becoming a Franciscan (or a Benedictine, Carmelite, Dominican, or any other). It is enough to confess the Lordship of Christ as Saviour, Friend and Brother, and to be baptized into the fellowship of the universal Church in the name of the Father, Son, and Holy Spirit, feeding upon the eucharistic body and blood of Christ, and living in love and compassion towards humankind. This means taking the gospel as your rule of life without getting involved with the machinery or complication of any monastic pattern.

Indeed, this was Francis' own idea, for in his day much monasticism had become lax, corrupt, and bureaucratic. His first Rule was the simple linking together of gospel texts to guide the friars in a charismatic but disciplined manner. His desire was to map out a pilgrimage pattern in order to make the ancient gospel contemporary for his day, asking new questions of old gospel principles. He came up with the threefold Franciscan Order, and it met the needs of his followers, directing a newly awakened evangelical fervour into disciplined channels of love, joy, and peace towards God and humankind.

We are faced today with the task of creating viable ways of translating the gospel's relevance to contemporary need. Identification with the vision, influence, and fellowship of Francis is one of the primary ways of accomplishing this. Because of the radical nature of Francis' perspective, there will always be tensions, questionings, and a desire for more profound reform and dedication in any Franciscan group, but there is also the fellowship of the community of love, based on the gospel, and a current awareness and participation in the world's sorrows, moving towards healing and reconciliation.

THE SOCIETY OF ST FRANCIS

This is the only part of this book which may appear parochial, but my desire is to present a concrete example of how the Third Order functions in one part of the Church.

The Society of St Francis is a body of Christians within the Anglican communion who seek to live out the gospel of Christ in the spirit of St Francis of Assisi. All who participate in this life do so because of a response to an interior vocation – a call of God. The framework and disciplines of such a life enable them to give themselves more fully to the sanctifying work of the Holy Spirit in the context of the love of God. There are particular emphases in the Franciscan life, the keynotes of which are humility, love, and joy, with the disciplines of prayer, study, and work.

The *First Order* consists of men (The Society of St Francis/SSF) and women (The Community of St Francis/CSF) who live in community under a Rule based on the traditional vows of poverty, celibacy, and obedience.

The *Second Order* consists of women (The Community of St Clare/CSCl) called to an enclosed life of contemplative prayer, with the same vows.

The *Third Order* (Tertiary Order/TO) consists of men and women, ordained and lay, married and single, between the ages of eighteen and sixty (for admission), who believe God is calling them to live a Franciscan vocation in the world. These are the Anglican counterpart today of the original Brothers and Sisters of Penance founded by St Francis. This life is lived in the midst of a secular calling, yet under rule, with a vow of lifelong intention.

There is also a large group of *Companions* who do not feel they want to commit themselves to the Third Order for various reasons, but who belong firmly to the Franciscan family, who meet together regularly, and share in some of the activities of the rest of the family as they are able.

Aspirants to the Third Order, if accepted, undergo a postulancy of at least six months, keeping an experimental rule before being admitted to the noviciate, which lasts two years, leading to profession with lifelong intention.

Tertiaries have a counsellor or spiritual director who guides them in the life of prayer towards the mature realization of their spiritual potential. The director is chosen at the postulancy and is approved by the provincial chaplain. With the help of his/her director, every tertiary draws up a personal rule of life that expresses the three Franciscan ways of service – prayer, study, and work. The rule of life affirms the values of poverty, chastity, and obedience adapted to life in the world, and encourages the growth of the Franciscan principles of humility, love, and joy.

The postulants and novices are in the care of a novice counsellor, who is an experienced tertiary, and they meet quarterly for spiritual fellowship and reflection on the rule. Members of the Third Order pledge the keeping of their rule for one year, and the pledge is renewed annually at a tertiary meeting. This renewed pledge is the basis of membership, and the bond that unites all members of the Order. It is also a safeguard against merely nominal membership, and promotes mutual fellowship and love. It also provides a dynamic sense of movement and change within the stability of rule and renewal.

A Franciscan friar must be something of a free spirit – as I was recently described in a book review in an evangelical magazine! Perhaps this is why, even in writing up the last few paragraphs, I begin to feel the constraints of any rules or obligations which are added to the gospel. When the rule of life is handed to the sister or brother upon profession, I want to cry out: 'If he/she has the gospel, there is no need for additional regulations!' But another part of me realizes the need and importance of guidance as to the meaning of the written Gospels, for they too are one step away from the immediacy of life in and with Jesus, and they were written decades after the events they record. And when I read the *Principles* and *Rule of Life* of sisters and brothers of the First Order, and the similar documents which answer for the Second and Third Orders, it is clear that they are interpreting gospel principles for our day.[13]

Indeed, it can become exciting for the prospective Third Order member to compose his or her rule of life with the help of a counsellor, for the dynamic of the Holy Spirit interacts with the postulant's personal belief and life-style in a new and life-giving commitment. An illustration of the kind of rule that may emerge is given below as a guide for those who want to undertake such a commitment.

DRAWING UP A RULE OF LIFE

We cannot guide ourselves. The Holy Spirit is the true spiritual director, but within the body of Christ spiritual care, confession, and healing are among the charisms of the Spirit. Within the Third Order your novice counsellor may help you to draw up your rule, or you may choose your own soul friend. A rule of life for a tertiary may run something like this:

The Holy Eucharist. You should aim to receive holy communion on Sundays and Greater Festivals, and hope to include a weekday Eucharist if possible.

Penitence. Regular self-examination and meetings with your Director are commended, which may be followed by sacramental confession (at least before Christmas, Easter, and Pentecost), or personal discussion seeking counsel and advice.

Prayer and Meditation. Definite daily periods should be set aside for the daily office, and an evolving discipline of meditation under guidance. The minimum time may be stated, so that it can be kept without strain.

Life-style. This will vary greatly depending upon the age, outlook, and temperament of the tertiary. It should include some physical exercise, commitment to study, and spiritual awareness. Matters of fasting and diet, disciplines of tobacco and alcohol, and the use of money are all involved. Also included are 'works of mercy' such as visiting the sick, lonely, or imprisoned, and financial help to individuals or some reconciling/helping agency such as Amnesty International, Christian Aid, Tear Fund, etc. The whole matter of tithing and its allocation may apply.

Retreat. Tertiaries should make an annual retreat – it may be a Third Order retreat or a group or private one. If for family or health reasons this is not possible, then a number of Quiet Days should be listed.

Study. This is mentioned under *Life-Style*, but separate attention should be given to it, depending upon individual capacity and time. Bible study comes first, with commentary aids. It is worth taking advice, reading reviews, and sharing in group discussion. Study also involves the Christian learning a little about all the great intellectual disciplines to broaden and deepen one's understanding of God's world.

Simplicity. The distribution of one's goods was a primary act in early Franciscan life, and the principle of simplicity is relative to one's personal and family responsibilities. The sharing of what is retained should be borne in mind, involving hospitality, provision of transport if you have a car, and going back to your bicycle!

Work. If you have employment, be thankful! But quite apart from asking if your work is compatible with your Christian profession, it is necessary to allow the gospel to be expressed in daily work through attitudes, punctuality, honesty, and open-hearted humour. The love of God can be manifested in the cleaning of windows, looking after children, delivering the milk, or caring for patients.

Obedience. Seeing your counsellor/director twice a year should be a matter of obedience. Consideration of obedience involves humility, trust, discipline, and humour, and you should reflect on the obedience owed to love. Such reflection will also indicate your attitude to authority, responsibility, and spontaneity, and be a fruitful area for self-evaluation.

Fellowship. As a tertiary, it is presumed that worship in your local church and fellowship with other Franciscans is part of your ongoing Christian life. Contact and friendship with wider groups and other faiths are also encouraged, to keep open all the human channels of communication at every level.

It is better not to aim too high, for falling down often means discouragement and unnecessary guilt – and that is certainly *not* what it is about! If you set your sights somewhat lower than your expectations, then it will be an encouragement to feel that the rule of life is a help and guide, and can be adjusted accordingly and realistically, depending on changing circumstances.

THE FIRST TERTIARIES

The first tertiary fraternity was established at Florence in 1221, during Francis' visit there with Cardinal Hugolino. Almost immediately, the new penitents established a hospital there which they maintained themselves.

Among the first of the group were the merchant Luchesio and his wife Buona Donna. He is called the Blessed Luchesio, and is thought of as the patron of the Third Order.

He had been a prosperous wool-merchant and politican in Cagiano in the Senese, of the Guelf or papal party. In those days he shrewdly held back his wool stocks in times of abundance, to sell them in times of scarcity.

When Siena fell into the hands of the Ghibellines, Luchesio and his wife fled to Poggibonsi in Florentine territory, and there, as a result of exile and meeting with Francis, they underwent radical conversion. Their story is of interest to us not only because they are reputed to be the first penitent tertiaries in the new Order, but also because of the conversion of their life-style, which serves as a pattern for tertiaries.

They distributed their wealth to the poor, keeping back only four acres of land, taking the habit of penitents. Then they took in sick and unfortunate people, fed them from their vegetable plot, and nursed them to health.

When money and food ran out, Luchesio went begging from door to door, with great success. A typical story is of Buona Donna, the 'gracious lady', looking out of the house one day and seeing Luchesio coming with one sick man on his back and another on their donkey. Father Cuthbert tells their story with its moving conclusion:

> Thus in incessant service for the needy and in self-denying love of God and their neighbour, Luchesio and his wife came to the life eternal. They had been true companions in life and they kept their companionship in death. Both fell mortally sick about the same time. Buona Donna prayed she might not out-live her husband and her prayer was heard. Luchesio rose from his bed to assist his wife in her last agony; then he returned to bed and died also: 'in death they were not divided'.[14]

Lord God,
who opened the eyes of the blessèd Francis to the vocation of
those you call to serve you in the world;
grant such grace to members of the Third Order, that being
crucified with Christ,
they may show forth among all people the radiance of his
risen life;
Through Jesus Christ our Lord. Amen.

12 ❧ *Franciscan Praying*

A WIDE SPECTRUM

As Franciscan spirituality is a particular way of believing and experiencing the gospel, so Franciscan praying is a distinctive application of Francis' charism to the life of prayer. It affects such a life at all levels, setting the creative genius of Francis within the context of biblical teaching and experience. Whatever the level of prayer, the Franciscan dimension imparts an immediacy that combines both mind and heart, avoiding intellectual dryness on the one hand and crude emotionalism on the other.

PRAYING WITH NATURE

Francis never used the term nature (*natura*) as an abstract, intellectual concept, but kept before him the biblical picture of God's creation, all the particular parts and creatures in the natural order manifesting the divine harmony and love.[1] He did not preach sermons or give lessons on the place of nature in the economy of God, but simply accepted and entered into the interrelated web of life that he found in the created world and among its creatures.

His biographers, especially those writing 'official' lives, like Celano and Bonaventure, often describe Francis' relation with creation and his affection for creatures in a style which sounds didactic, as if we are to learn lessons instead of entering experientially into creation in the way that Francis did, with all his spontaneity and joy, melancholy and pain − influenced by the beauty or the cruelty that he found before him.

Some of the non-official sources[2] portray the immediacy of wonder, joy, sorrow, and ecstasy of genuine Franciscan experience, but even Celano and Bonaventure are dazzled by the genius of Francis, and though they cannot help applying teaching from various incidents, the spontaneous dynamic of Francis continually shines through.

Bonaventure says that Francis was filled with great affection for all creatures because he realized that we all come from the same creative source in God. Then he brings together a whole set of incidents in which Francis' love for creatures causes him to enter into fellow feeling with them, resulting in reciprocal communion.

There are a number of lamb stories, because they always reminded Francis of the Lamb of God sacrificed for our redemption. There are also stories of the affectionate hare that he liberated at Greccio, the rabbit he embraced on Lake Trasimene, the ecstasy while holding a water-bird on Lake Piediluco, and the brother fish he replaced in the same lake. These, with many other bird and beast stories, showed Francis to be innocent, like pre-fallen Adam in paradise. Bonaventure saw in Francis a reversal of the fall, able to relate to creatures because he was both redeemed and saintly in his innocence:

> We should have the greatest reverence, therefore, for St Francis' loving compassion which had such wonderful charm that it could bring savage animals into subjection and tame the beasts of the forest, training those which were tame already and claiming obedience from those which had rebelled against fallen mankind.[3]

Both Bonaventure and Celano have recourse to their Augustinian, Neoplatonic perspective in commending Francis' awareness of the divine pattern and harmony in creation. But there is much more to it than that:

> In everything beautiful, he saw him who is beauty itself, and he followed his Beloved everywhere by his likeness imprinted on creation; of all creation he made a ladder by which he may mount up and embrace Him who is all-desirable. By the power of his extraordinary faith he tasted the Goodness which is the source of all in each and every created thing, as in so many rivulets. He seemed to perceive a divine harmony in the interplay of powers and faculties given by God to his creatures ...[4]

Francis lived in a constant atmosphere of prayer in the Holy Spirit. It was not simply that he observed evidence of design and harmony, or that he learned and appreciated the goodness and purpose of God's mercy, but he actually experienced life, light, and love in the Spirit, and often became enraptured and ecstatic in the contemplation of the natural order:

> Who would be able to narrate the sweetness he enjoyed while contemplating in creatures the wisdom of their Creator, his power and his goodness? Indeed, he was very often filled with a wonderful and ineffable joy from this consideration while he looked upon the sun, while he beheld the moon, and while he gazed upon the stars and the firmament.[5]

113

This was no exceptional experience for Francis, for right from the beginning he was touched ecstatically by the Spirit:

> Already beneath his secular garb he wore a religious spirit and, withdrawing to solitary places, he was often admonished by a visitation of the Holy Spirit. For he was carried away and enticed by that perfect sweetness which poured over him with such abundance from the very beginning that it never departed from him as long as he lived.[6]

There is a giftlike quality in all this. It cannot be learned from books or studied in theological courses. But exposure to its immediacy can increase its influence. My own childhood experience touches that of Francis at so many points, and my ongoing pilgrimage confirms the genuineness of my intuitive awareness.

If you have had childhood experiences of mystery and wonder in nature, don't let them 'fade into the light of common day', but get out into solitary and beautiful places – allow your spirit to be exposed to light and darkness, sunshine and rain, sea and forest, mountain and valley. Let your spirit become lost in contemplation of the natural order, in the changing cycle of seasons, in the height and depth of natural manifestations of loveliness and awe.

The more you do this, the more you will open yourself to the intuitive insights of natural contemplation, and the more you will unblock the natural channels of communication, so that the Holy Spirit can flood into your mundane life and lift you on to a new and higher plane of awareness. It will not be an escape or flight from the 'real world', but a profound and increasing awareness that there is another level of reality that will abide when this one has perished. This kind of Franciscan praying is living in the light of eternity and of God.

PRAYING WITH SCRIPTURE

People associate the placing of oneself within the text of Scripture with the Ignatian exercises, but that tradition is itself an expression of the Holy Spirit's interior influence in the believer's approach to Scripture.

The Holy Spirit inspired the authors of Scripture as they wrote, and the same Spirit inspires the believer who approaches the sacred text.

The Franciscan attitude to Scripture is more of an inspirational than a dogmatic one. That is not to say that there is a low view of objective inspiration and authority, for the Franciscan understanding of Scripture is that of the wider Church. But there is an inspirational attitude that readily understands the truth that 'Scripture is inspired because it inspires'.

There is, of course, a subjective danger in such an attitude, as is exemplified in the early Franciscan practice of opening the Bible or missal three times for guidance. The superstitious abuse of such a practice is clear in the story of the man who opened the Bible at random and placed his finger on the text that reads: 'And Judas went out and hanged himself.' That was not an appropriate word, so he tried again: 'Go thou and do likewise'! Perplexed, he gave it one more try: 'What thou doest, do quickly'!

In spite of such possible abuse, Francis and his first two friars found the guidance they needed in opening the Bible three times, and at La Verna, Leo opened the Scripture to the story of Christ's passion, in confirmation of Francis' intuition that this was to be the confrontation that was immediately before him.[7]

Francis lived within the letter of Scripture so that the spirit of Scripture was realized in his experience. He so lived in the Gospels that he acted out incidents of story, parable, and miracle, and they became part of the pattern of his own life. As John Moorman writes:

> As he could enter, with shepherds and magi, into the stable of Bethlehem and kneel in wonder before the crib, so he could stand at the foot of the cross, with Mary and John, and live through all the agony of those hours. It was to this end that he prayed, on La Verna, that he might feel in his own body and soul 'the pain that thou, sweet Lord, didst bear in the hour of thy most bitter passion', and could teach others to pray that they might 'die for love of thy love as thou didst deign to die for love of my love'.[8]

There were many among the Spiritual friars of the Marches of Ancona who constantly lived in simple conformity to the Gospels. John of Fermo was one, who became John of La Verna, living in a supernatural ardour that lasted three years. Ubertino of Casale also meditated long on Mount La Verna, as a result of which he wrote in his *Arbor Vitae Crucifixae*:

> Jesus made me feel, in an extraordinary way, that I was with

him in every action of his life — that I was, first, the ass; then the ox; then the crib; then the hay on which he lay; then the servant attending him; then one of his parents; and, lastly, the Child Jesus himself. He took me with him when he fled into Egypt, and to the temple on his return, and to Nazareth with his mother. In a strange manner I knew that I was with him at his baptism, in the desert, in the course of his preaching, and constantly in treacheries, desertions, insults and injuries.

Bonaventure commends the typically Franciscan emphasis on the human life of Jesus as the royal road to deeper participation in God. Consideration of the life of Jesus means entering in contemplative imagination into every moment of his birth, life, and death. In a *Letter to a Poor Clare*, he writes:

Draw near, dear handmaiden, with loving feet to Jesus wounded, to Jesus crowned with thorns, to Jesus fastened to the gibbet of the cross; and be not content, as the blessed apostle Thomas was, merely to see in his hands the print of the nails or to thrust your hand into his side; but rather go right in, through the opening in his side, to the very heart of Jesus where, transformed by most burning love for Christ, held by the nails of divine love, pierced by the lance of profound charity, and wounded by the sword of deep compassion, you will know no other wish or desire or hope of consolation except to die with Christ upon the cross, so that you can say with S. Paul: 'I am crucified with Christ ... I live; yet not I, but Christ liveth in me.'[9]

The Franciscan is not simply a spectator, but a participant, hearing the words, sharing the life, dying and rising with Jesus. The Christian faith is therefore not only a catechism of doctrine that must be learned by rote, or part of a liturgical exercise or ritual, but a living experience in which the Jesus of the Gospels becomes the Christ of experience. He is the Saviour, Friend and Brother of daily life.

Another aspect of living out the gospel narrative is that shown in the poetry of Jacopone da Todi. His response is poured out in the famous *Stabat Mater Dolorosa*. After contemplating the sufferings of Mary at the foot of the cross, there is the plea that the believer might share in them, standing near Our Lady, feeling in the heart the sorrows she endured.

PRAYING WITH THE LITURGY

It was expected that all Franciscans should attend mass, receive holy communion, and share in the liturgical services of the Church. Those friars and sisters who were not literate could share in the canonical hours, memorizing and repeating the basic prayers.

In his private prayers, Francis would often be overcome by the divine presence, in trance and rapture, and often with sighs, tears, and groaning. But when he worshipped liturgically or in church, he would observe a discipline of body and mind so as not to give offence or disclose the divine intoxication that would smite and possess him in the woods and in solitude.[10]

The Franciscan movement was not a monastic Order in which the primary work of God (*opus Dei*) was the chanting and offering of the divine office in choir. The Franciscan cloister was the world, and the canonical hours were often observed standing next to the Franciscan donkey in the rain on an evangelistic journey.[11]

But the Franciscan friar or sister was as much a praying member of the body of Christ as the monk in his abbey, and worship was not simply the individual prayers of a mendicant or sister, but a participation in the communal offering of catholic worship throughout the day and night on behalf of all creation. The Poor Clares did of course offer the canonical hours in choir, and as time went on large convents were built and the friars' life took on a more monastic style.

Liturgical prayer and worship is offered to God the Father, the Creator, through God the Son, the Redeemer, and in God the Holy Spirit, the Sanctifier and Life-Giver. Modern Franciscan liturgical prayer is part of the whole offering of prayer throughout the whole Church:

> We are only able to pray because we are in the Spirit: the Spirit of Christ, the Spirit of the whole Church, the Spirit present in each baptised person. 'We do not know how to pray as we ought, but the Spirit intercedes for us' — the Spirit intercedes for the saints according to the will of God. In the Spirit, we can offer true prayer to God, for 'when we cry Abba! Father! it is the Spirit of God affirming to our spirit'. It is the Spirit who unites the whole Church and brings us through the Redeemer to the Creator.[12]

Franciscan life is always at the heart of the Church, and cannot exist outside the Church. Its centre is the life and proclamation of Christ in word and sacrament, and the Franciscan always finds himself or herself feeding upon Christ in Scripture and Eucharist, and then moving out into the world to proclaim the good news and alleviate human suffering.

Francis may have found it more difficult than we do to separate personal and liturgical prayer, for as Bonaventure says:

> He burned with love for the Sacrament of our Lord's Body with all his heart, and was lost in wonder at the thought of such condescending love, such loving condescension. He received Holy Communion often and so devoutly that he roused others to devotion too. The presence of the Immaculate Lamb used to take him out of himself, so that he was often lost in ecstasy.[13]

PRAYING AT ALL TIMES

Prayer should be the very atmosphere of the Franciscan's life. Celano says that when secular persons or business would disturb Francis, 'he would interrupt his prayers rather than end them, and return to them again in his innermost being'.

If certain people came, and Francis knew it was not right for him to speak with them, he would say to the friars: 'Thy word have I hidden in my heart, that I may not sin against thee,' and they would courteously dismiss them or deal with them privately, so that Francis could continue his profound communion with God.[14]

Different situations would elicit different kinds of praying. Guidance would sometimes come directly and powerfully, sometimes after prolonged prayer and fasting, and sometimes as in the following childlike story of need for direction.

One day Masseo was walking ahead of Francis in Tuscany and came to a threefold signpost to Siena, Florence, and Arrezzo. 'Father, which road should we take?' asked Masseo. Francis looked to God, and then commanded Masseo to twirl himself around, which he did until he became quite giddy.

Then suddenly Francis cried: 'Stand still! Don't move!' And then: 'What direction are you facing?' 'Towards Siena,' replied Masseo with dizziness. 'That is the road God wants us to take,' concluded Francis.

As a result of this, they arrived at Siena, reconciled a fighting band of citizens, and were received with joy by the bishop. The story ends by saying that Masseo 'understood with certainty that the Spirit of divine wisdom and grace guided Francis in all his actions'.[15]

When I first read Bonaventure's comments on Francis' prayerful affection for, and attitude to, living creatures, especially to the lamb which had been killed by a vicious sow, it reminded me of the lamb which became for me the occasion of contemplative prayer.

I had been living in solitude for nearly six months on the Lleyn Peninsula, facing the Island of Bardsey, with mountain sheep scattered over the hillside above the sea. On Maundy Thursday I climbed to the top of the hill Anelog, where there was a flat, exposed area. There I marked fourteen stones with the 'Stations of the Cross', and a fifteenth mound of stones surmounted with an empty wooden cross for the resurrection.

So, on Good Friday I ascended the hill to walk the stations from 2.00 p.m. to 3.00 p.m., following Jesus' way of sorrows to Calvary. It was windy, dark, and menacing as I climbed the hill, and when I got to the top I found, in the midst of the fifteen stations, a dead lamb. It had been attacked, blinded, and killed by the ravens, and as I looked at its small, white woolly body among the rocks I was moved to tears, and said 'O Lamb of God, who takes away the sins of the world, have mercy upon us ...'

I prayed the stations of the cross through the next hour, and during that time the wind dropped, the clouds parted, and the sun broke through. The dead lamb remained in the midst of the stones, but I was able to move from the death to the risen life of Jesus in the Scriptures and in the events of that day, which were all taken up into my prayer.

Francis' practice was to take his whole life to God in prayer, so that nothing was deemed impossible. With eleven brothers, poor and unknown, he prayed and felt impelled to journey to the great Pope Innocent III for his approval.

Some of the sources reveal that the pope's immediate response was negative and haughty. But prayerful trust and persistence on Francis' part moved Cardinal John of St Paul to speak for Francis to the pope and cardinals.

As a result, the pope said: 'My son, pray to Christ that he may show us his will through you. When we are sure of that, we can grant your request without fear.' Then Bonaventure asserts the priority of prayer: 'Francis immediately gave himself up completely to prayer; and as a reward for his fervour it was made known to him what he should say, and simultaneously it was revealed to the pope what he should think.'[16]

Because of the power of prayer, the pope approved Francis' gospel rule for the friars, and gave them a mission to preach repentance and the word of God without interference.

FRANCIS' PERSONAL PRAYER AND MEDITATION

The reason why Francis was so attracted to the hermit life was that he was enamoured of God, longing to be united with Christ in his passion and resurrection. But he obeyed the will of God to live an apostolic life of preaching, healing, and guiding his Order. But always he prayed:

> No human tongue could describe the passionate love with which Francis burned for Christ, his Spouse; he seemed to be completely absorbed by the fire of divine love like a glowing coal. The moment he heard the love of God being mentioned, he was aroused immediately and so deeply moved and inflamed that it seemed as if the deepest chord in his heart had been plucked by the words ... He loved Christ so fervently and Christ returned his love so intimately that he seemed to have his Saviour before his eyes continually, as he once privately admitted to his companions.[17]

And as Thomas of Celano said:

> His safest haven was prayer; not prayer of a single moment, or idle or presumptuous prayer, but prayer of long duration, full of devotion, serene in humility. If he began late he would scarcely finish before morning. Walking, sitting, eating, or drinking, he was always intent upon prayer. He would go alone to pray at night in churches abandoned and located in deserted places.[18]

If we ask what method or technique Francis used in his prayer and meditation, there is no clear answer. Indeed, he would think such a question very odd and perhaps sacrilegious. To him, prayer was not so much the human lifting of the heart to God, as being apprehended by the Holy Spirit — a human response to the divine initiative. We live in days of psychological techniques, so it is well for us to keep the divine sovereignty in prayer before our eyes and hearts.

Spontaneity was the hallmark of Francis' personal prayer, but it could serve to discourage us if we look to him as a saint elevated beyond our reach on the heights of holiness. Spontaneous and affective devotion sprung up from a disciplined life, and we see that there were certain ascetic attitudes that made him open and available, so that when God was ready, he could flood Francis' being with the divine love. He sought beautiful, natural places of solitude, like the woods, lakes, islands, mountains, and caves of Subasio and La Verna, and often quiet churches where he could pour out his heart. We have seen that he did this from earliest days, and in secret, so that he could abandon himself to God with cries, sighing, weeping, and prostration. But if anyone did stumble upon his private prayer, they were profoundly affected. As the *Legend of the Three Companions* reports:

> One day he was roaming about alone near the church of Saint Mary of the Angels, weeping and lamenting aloud. A certain God-fearing man heard him and, thinking he must be ill, asked pityingly the reason for his distress. Francis replied: 'I weep for the passion of my Lord Jesus Christ; and I should not be ashamed to go weeping through the whole world for his sake.' Then the other man fell to crying and lamenting with him.[19]

We may feel that such spontaneity is too much for our inhibited and shrunken souls, or such discipline is too demanding for our soft and flabby bodies, but if we are to allow Francis' example to guide us, we can look to him in principle and allow his influence to lend fire to our attempts.

Let me offer a simple method based on the night he spent at the invitation of Bernard of Quintivalle, who secretly watched him, and as a result joined him as a friar.

When Francis thought Bernard was asleep, he quietly got up and placed himself in a physical attitude of prayer, at times gazing upward and raising his hands, sometimes weeping and entranced, repeating through the night: 'My God and my All.'

The *Fioretti* tells this story movingly, saying that through the night God showed Francis his divine compassion for a lost and needy world by giving Christ as Saviour, and that he would anoint Francis with the Holy Spirit and use him for the salvation of many souls. Francis' response was one of repentance for his unworthiness, and wonder and adoration of spirit. Out of the depths of such prayer came the rhythmic repetition of the words, as a Christian mantra: 'My God and my All.'[20]

My own practice, following this and other stories of Francis at prayer, follows this pattern:

Posture. Francis found solitude and quietness, then he placed himself in the posture for prayer. As we grow in prayer we can devote more and more time, so our posture needs to be relaxed and free from tension. If you can sit in the classic, cross-legged posture, then do so. I use a prayer stool upon which one can sit for more than two hours with no problem, but a straight back on a stool or a hard-backed chair will serve just as well. Francis raised his eyes and his hands at times, and at other times he meditated while walking, riding on a donkey, or stretched on the ground, on a rock, or under a tree. There is great variation, but stillness of mind and relaxation of all parts of the body are a prerequisite for periods of meditation.

Respiration. If prayer is a response of spirit to Spirit, it is well to remember that the Hebrew word *ruach* means *spirit, wind,* or *breath,* and so does the Greek word *pneuma.* This indicates that not only is the human spirit 'inspired' or breathed into by the Holy Spirit, but that the physical action of breathing is important in the discipline of meditation. It is worth learning a simple breathing pattern at the beginning, so that it becomes second nature and we can then forget about it when it carries our rhythmic prayers.

Repetition. The *Fioretti* story shows us that Francis used to repeat phrases or parts of Scripture or psalms, just as the blind man repeatedly called: 'Jesus, Son of David, have mercy on me,' or as the angelic beings cried 'day and night without ceasing' before the throne of God.[21] The Aramaic term *Maranatha* is used by many in repetition, as is the classic Jesus Prayer: 'Lord Jesus Christ, Son of God, have mercy on me, a sinner.' These may be said rhythmically, with regular breathing or with the heartbeat.

Visualization. Here, what we have said under 'Praying with Scripture' applies. It is not just observing Scripture, but participating in Scripture, getting into the very marrow of Scripture in order to understand it from within. It may also be the visualization of an aspect of God's nature — his love, his holiness, his faithfulness, so that the heart is touched and the will moved. Bonaventure expects such to happen: 'O human heart, you are harder than any hardness of rocks, if at the recollection of such great expiation you are not struck with terror, nor moved with compassion nor shattered with compunction nor softened with devoted love.'[22]

Contemplation. Let me make a distinction between meditation and contemplation. *Meditation* is initiated by the meditator, though the Holy Spirit moves, guides, and illumines in the process. But *contemplation* is that level of prayer that is 'in the Spirit', and gazes upon God in adoration and perhaps ecstasy — a foretaste of the unitive life of heaven.

Returning from La Verna in great weakness, and riding on a donkey, Francis and his friars passed through the village of Borgo San Sepolcro. The crowds rushed to greet the saint, pulling and dragging him, tearing pieces of his habit, and crying out for prayer or in joy. Francis was rapt in contemplation during this time, and much later in the journey he asked when they would reach the village of Borgo. 'His mind was fixed on the glory of heaven,' says Bonaventure, 'and so he had lost all track of changes of place or time or people. His companions knew from their own experience that this often happened to him.'[23]

It is God's business to grant these glimpses of the unitive life. The gift of contemplation belongs to what used to be called 'infused' prayer, and is not the result of ascetic disciplines, technique, or psychological methods. It is wholly God's work. But in order for it to happen, we must make ourselves ready, be open to his call, and give ourselves to prayer, Scripture, and meditation.

There are times when I am digging in the vegetable garden, perhaps at sunrise, when I feel the gentle and sensitive approach of the Holy Spirit. I can then continue the manual work in a rhythmic and gentle manner, allowing the Lord to fill my mind and heart with his love; or I may feel that I must lay my spade down and turn aside to a quiet solitude, allowing God to take me where he will. It is easier to do this if you live in solitude, but as Francis found, it is possible almost anywhere:

Francis would never let any call of the Spirit go unanswered; when he experienced it, he would make the most of it and enjoy the consolation afforded him in this way for as long as God permitted it. If he was on a journey and felt the near approach of God's Spirit, he would stop and let his companions go on, while he drank in the joy of this new inspiration; he refused to offer God's grace an ineffectual welcome (cf. 2 Cor 6. 1). He was often taken right out of himself in a rapture of contemplation, so that he was lost in ecstasy and had no idea what was going on about him, while he experienced things which were beyond all human understanding.[24]

Part of the Franciscan discipline is to find some solitude from time to time, for in spite of the fact that the Christian press advertises 'instant prayer for busy people', such promotion must be taken with a block of salt! It is like the advertisements for French (or Latin) without time, trouble, or tears. It's simply not true!

There is a place for 'arrow prayers', and God will meet with you instantly in a desperate situation if you cry out: 'Lord, save me!' But that is for emergencies, and when the emergency is over, then it is time to develop a devotional life of prayer and contemplation. And the deeper you go, the more necessary it becomes.

Francis knew that when he was burdened with the sins and sorrows of the world, when he needed strength for proclamation and healing, when he had to confront dark and demonic powers, then he needed solitude, and sometimes that meant the silent hours of the night.

After such times, he would return to the friars, and though he would endeavour to hide it, they would see such a transformation of light and glory that he appeared physically like Moses, whose face shone, or like Christ, who was transfigured on the mountain. On one occasion the bishop of Assisi went into Francis' cell in the enclosure when he was lost in prayer. So great was the glory that the bishop was seized with trembling, became paralysed and dumb, and was ejected backwards and thrown out of the enclosure.[25]

We conclude this chapter with one of the sayings from *The Book of the Lover and the Beloved* by the Franciscan Ramon Lull:

The Lover said to the Beloved, 'You who fill the sun with splendour, fill my heart with love.' The Beloved answered, 'If you did not possess fullness of love, your eyes would not have shed those tears, nor would you have come to this place to see him who loves you.'[26]

God our loving Father:
Our hearts are cold until warmed by your Holy Spirit, and
   our prayers lifeless until imbued by your sacred fire;
Stir us up to prayer and action, that our words and lives
   may incarnate the love of Christ;
For your praise and our world's good. Amen.

13 🌿 *Ecology and Reconciliation*

CELT, CHRISTIAN, AND FRANCISCAN

I am a Celt. I am a Christian. I am a Franciscan friar. These are three solid reasons why I have always experienced a feeling relationship with the earth, the created order, and our common humanity. It is a sense of sacredness, reverence for life, compassion for all sentient creatures – and it is all bound up together in one package.

I sometimes have a friendly argument with one of our brothers. The point at issue is that I maintain that there are general characteristics which pertain to certain groups of peoples or nations, and he denies it (of course, we press our claims too far, to enliven the argument!). I begin from my own perception, for my Welshness makes me affirm affinity with the Scots and the Irish, and I am not afraid to assent to the primacy of feeling, emotion, and intuition over *ratio* and cold, objective logic in approaching and solving problems. This can be overstated, of course, and there are particular exceptions.

Today, Celtic spirituality is receiving the attention it deserves, with its mystical relationship with the earth and its implications for ecology.[1] I would not want to deny the nature mysticism in much English poetry, exemplified in Wordsworth's *Tintern Abbey*. But there is a distinctive difference of approach in the cool charm, gentleness, and courtesy of English spirituality as found in Lady Julian of Norwich or the *Cloud of Unknowing*, and the fiery and emotional poetry and preaching of the Spaniard St John of the Cross and the Italian Jacopone da Todi.

It is not that one is *better* than another, but they are *different*, and contribute diverse strands in what must ultimately be a holistic and complete approach, needing the multi-faceted understanding of many traditions.

It is difficult for me to separate my Celtic inheritance from the fact that I live in the life of Christ and in the light of St Francis. My Celtic roots are deeper than my individual life. Even as a child, I felt 'larger than myself', involved in some mysterious, embracing, reciprocal dialogue with nature. When I later began to read mystical writers in my teens and twenties, and then writers in the Buddhist, Taoist, and Hindu traditions, I *recognized* what they were saying because I had already *experienced* the mystic coinherence of spirit and matter and the interrelated web of existence as a child. Of course, I could not have used or recognized the words then, but my childhood experience lit up the later descriptions. Before I had set eyes on St Francis' *Canticle of Brother Sun*, I could say that the sun rose and set in my own soul; the moon waxed and waned in my changing moods; the sea ebbed and flowed in my own emotions; the cycle of the seasons and the fertility of the earth were all patterned within my body and psyche.

It was at twelve years of age that I began, consciously, to follow in the way of Christ. In an evangelical conversion experience, he became Saviour, Friend, and Brother. It was not difficult to relate redemption to creation, for it began for me with a sense of wonder, and then went on to a need for redemption. Original innocence was my experience before a sense of sin!

Unfortunately, in Wales, as in the rest of Celtic Britain, a sort of negative puritanism was imposed on to the Christ-experience (Nonconformist in Wales, Presbyterian in Scotland, Roman Catholic in Ireland!). But I could never really imbibe enough of this puritanism to cause me to lose sight of my childhood inheritance.

The Bible came to my aid in affirming the glory of God in creation, and my Pentecostal friends helped me to believe and experience the Holy Spirit, active today and in our midst.

Then the introduction to Franciscan spirituality brought me into the dimension of Francis' intoxication with the beauty of creation and the redeeming love of Christ. Perhaps the Italian and the Celtic share a family likeness in nature as well as grace!

This is not something that happened simply in my childhood, or a decade or two ago, but something that invades and inebriates my present existence.

Over the last three years, I have been exploring the hermit life on the grounds of Tymawr Convent, in Wales. During the last month, the students of Usk Agricultural College have initiated the planting of a thousand sapling trees here – Dogwood, Guelder, Blackthorn, Spindle, Hawthorn, Wayfaring, Ash, Lime, Cherry, Oak ...

After planting about six hundred, they left the rest to Martin, the convent gardener. So I have spent three mornings planting about a hundred and thirty, with great joy. Also, this morning, after my early prayer/meditation, I have been planting onion sets, beans, and cabbage plants. All this is not only the Franciscan dimension of manual work, but a caring for the earth, a planting in faith, and a meditation on dying and rising, bringing together creation and redemption in practical experience.

BENEDICT AND FRANCIS

Both Benedictine and Franciscan traditions possess an inbuilt reverence for the natural world, though the approach is different.

From the seventh century, Benedictine monasteries were established in Western Europe, and Benedict's *Rule* contains a threefold pattern of prayer, study, and manual work. The latter was a radical departure, for Greek and Roman scholars disdained manual labour as demeaning for a scholar or philosopher. Benedict ennobled manual work, and the tilling of the soil and care of animals were only part of the self-sufficiency of a monastery. The ideal was husbandry, responsible stewardship, and contributed much to the tradition of European agriculture.

Sean McDonagh quotes the American farmer Wendell Berry, who is campaigning for an end to industrial, high-technology, petroleum-based agriculture, which is debasing both the soil and the farmer. The Benedictine attitude of receiving the land as a gift, and of good husbandry, is expressed in Berry's words:

> To live we must daily break the body and shed the blood of creation. When we do this knowingly, lovingly, skillfully and reverently, it is a sacrament. When we do it ignorantly, greedily, clumsily and destructively it is a desecration. In such a descration we condemn ourselves to spiritual moral loneliness and others to want.[2]

McDonagh was a missionary for sixteen years in Mindanao, in the Republic of the Philippines, and now works among a tribal community called the T'boli. He says that it has been traditional to think of the Christian missionary as almost exclusively in a one-way communication stream. The task was to experience and learn the tenets of the Christian faith in the West, and to communicate it elsewhere. It would not be thought appropriate for the cultures of Africa, Asia, Latin America, or the Pacific to contribute to a new and revitalized understanding of the Christian faith.

At last, things are changing. Not only do indigenous peoples more and more control their own missions and churches, but the social, political, economic, and theological changes since the Second World War have shaken the Western world and the Western Church. There is dialogue and fraternal reciprocation between churches, missions, and nations, and the so-called First World is learning the truths dormant in its own faith, and from other world faiths in the countries in which missionaries serve.

After affirming the positive Benedictine approach to husbandry and stewardship, McDonagh still sees a Western desire to domesticate nature and bring it under control, and this belies 'a fear that

129

raw nature is unpredictable and capricious and can easily overpower human beings unless constant vigilance is maintained'.

While admiring the early Benedictine stewardship approach, he sees the decline of monastic life in increasing wealth and amassing land, so that monasteries became powerful economic and political centres, and the abbot began to look and act like a feudal lord.

Turning to the Franciscan tradition, he notes the difference. Francis was a nomad, his friars were on the move, with no possessions, living lightly on the earth. Francis thus abandoned any *homo faber* role for the brothers, so there is no agricultural tradition, and the natural world is not seen from a utilitarian perspective. Here there is no will to dominate or transform nature, but rather a fellowship approach, with a sense of joy, wonder, praise, and gratitude for the gift of all life. 'In his "Canticle of the Creatures"', says McDonagh, 'Francis shows a kinship with, and deep insight into, the heart of all creation — animate and inanimate — which is probably unique in the whole European experience.'

We shall turn to a consideration of the *Canticle* later, but it is worth noting that Francis' 'relationship' language with creatures is closer to the language of India, China, or the North American tradition than the European Christian approach.

We have noted that the Celtic spiritual tradition is at one with Francis in this, and that both these avoid *identifying* the divine with nature, as in *pantheism*, affirming rather *both* the immanence of God *within* nature and the transcendence of God *beyond* nature.

In Francis, there is a divine call to love, embracing both nature and neighbour in a healing and reconciling union that is the pattern both for ecology and political relationships throughout the world.

We must not drive a wedge between Benedict and Francis here, for both have creative insights into ecological wholeness and reverence for life, and both traditions later lapsed into laxity and corruption. For us it is significant to note that Francis lived at a time of particular turmoil and change, when the market-place mercantile economy took the place of a rural economy. Francis was born into the midst of it, and yet rejected his father's merchant values, life-style, and class and property consciousness.

Jesus had no place to lay his head, and Francis took from the earth only what was necessary for sustaining life, in contrast to a consumer society, with its obsessions for wealth, property, power, and deprivation of the poor.

Not only Franciscans, but across the Church and the denominations, Christians are beginning to wake up to the issues of peace and justice, with their attendant inequalities, but the disappointment expressed as a result of the 1992 Rio Summit reflects the disarray among wealthy and hypocritical Christians.

We are not concerned with total world-perspective matters, but often only with narrow national concerns, and these only as they affect the party-political ethos in a consumer society. The ecological crisis involves the poisoning of water, disposal of radioactive waste, thinning of the ozone layer, contamination of the atmosphere, depletion of topsoil, pollution of oceans, destruction of rain-forests, and the wholesale abuse of animals – apart from the continuing, though more subtle, danger of nuclear destruction since the disintegration of the Soviet Union.

It is not that the Christian tradition, and especially the Franciscan tradition, does not have creative insights and energies within its spirituality, but that the Western Christian perspective has been sidetracked. Exploitative Western colonialism and modern technological progress could have taken a path of responsible caring and sharing rather than manipulation and plunder. Neither missionary vision and activity nor technological progress are wrong in themselves – indeed we need the wisdom to harness them both – but abuse, exploitation, and plunder have landed us in a destructive situation.

A new creation theology, inextricably linked with the redeeming gospel of Christ, is required for the Church and the world. Sean McDonagh reaches back to the thirteenth-century Francis for such an insight:

The memory of Francis in our world today is a healing, reconciling and creative one. It inspires many people to become pacifists, to build a true fraternity among humans and to renounce war before it is too late for humanity and the Earth. It also inspires naturalists and ecologists to preserve nature untamed by humans. The protection of wilderness areas in our world today is essential for many reasons. Endangered species need a habitat if they are to survive and not become extinct. Experiencing the wilderness is an expanding and uplifting sensation for the human spirit. It draws us out beyond our own selves. An untamed environment, untouched by human beings, whether it is a vast ocean, a rain forest or a desert, points to the ultimate mystery at the heart of

131

the world which continually calls human beings to a deeper communion with the Earth and with God. Francis, the saint for all seasons, is particularly important today and so is a happy choice as the patron of ecologists.[3]

FRANCIS AND ECOLOGY

The word *ecology* derives from *oikos-logy*, which means, literally, a word about our home, or, to put it in more sophisticated language, environmental considerations. The whole world was home, or cloister, to Francis, and he loved every part of the cosmos and every creature. His loving compassion called forth a response from creatures and from fellow human beings, so a reciprocal and mutual relationship was created.

He never lost that innocence and sense of wonder that used to be part of childhood. As we set our agenda for environmental renewal, a re-education of children and adults in wonder should be high on the list of priorities.

What would some kind of environmental agenda look like? There would be tensions in its preparation, for as Christians and Franciscans we should look at our world as God's world, and at ourselves not as called to dominate, but to co-operate and work together with people of good will, religious or not, for the good of our planet. Here are some suggestions:

1 We need a new theological basis for thinking and acting. I have already quoted Sean McDonagh's *To Care for the Earth*. It is a book rich in theology and cosmology, and springs from a missionary and practical experience in which the sacramental practice of gospel and ecology run together. The theologian's theologian, Hans Küng, provides a sound basis in *Global Responsibility: In Search of a New World Ethic*. His far-reaching concerns are clear when he looks for: not just freedom, but also justice; not just equality, but also plurality; not just brotherhood, but also sisterhood; not just coexistence, but peace; not just productivity, but solidarity with the environment; not just toleration, but ecumenism.

2 We need to work openly in dialogue with the great world faiths and dedicated humanists, contributing our own insights and sharing those of others, confident in a Franciscan spirituality,

but seeing the *Poverello* and the hidden Christ wherever compassion is practised.

3 We need, personally and corporately, to work with agencies of
environmental renewal, and the peace and justice movements
across denominational and credal barriers, employing time and
talents in social and political concern wherever there is no compromise of the way of Christ and Francis.

4 We need to ask questions about the education of our children,
strengthening all the new approaches of environmental and
global awareness. We should seek to recover the sense of
wonder, joy, awe, and aesthetic enjoyment of all the creative
disciplines, integrating the scientific disciplines with music, art,
dance, and play.

5 We need to consolidate our Christ-centred faith, as Francis did.
This involves the promotion of a contemplative attitude, teaching
techniques of meditation, and integrating such an attitude into
every aspect of human life, secular and religious.

All these items need to be unpacked, but they provide a basis
from which we can develop a genuine ecological concern, in a
spirit of reconciliation and hope.

A TRUE UNDERSTANDING OF FRANCIS

When I first discovered Francis, I brought to my reflection on
his story my own preconceptions. In Francis, I expected to find
a convergence of two main lines of experience — first, an exuberant
and mystical response to creation; and second, an evangelical and
mystical response to the passion of Christ. These I did find, and I
am increasingly confirmed in my first approach. But I must admit
that I did not always find this twofold appreciation among others
who had seemingly read his story and taken his name.

First of all, there was a lack of appreciation of Francis' mystical
engagement with creation. He was thought of as a nature-lover, the
patron of domestic animals, cast as a statue bearing a bird-bath,
and moulded in plaster statues with a sentimental halo. I arrived
home in Swansea from the friary one day, and found that one
of our well-meaning neighbours had presented my mother with
a plastic wall-plaque of St Anthony of Padua holding a simpering
child in one arm and an arum lily in the other — in an appropriate

effeminate stance. It had been purchased in Swansea market! Nothing was further from the truth of either Anthony or Francis.

I returned to the sources, and found that Francis and the early friars experienced joy, ecstasy, inebriation, and wonder in their relationship with creation. Let me reproduce one out of the hundreds of illustrations from the primary sources.

If you read Celano's *First Life of St Francis*, around chapter twenty-nine you will find a loving, compassionate, reciprocal, and redemptive relationship described. The chapter itself contains a description of the inner and outer life of Francis, beginning with the words: 'It would take too long and be impossible to enumerate and gather together all the things the glorious Francis did and taught ...', and ending with a sensitive physical description of his appearance, leading to a prayerful description of his holiness. And in the middle of the chapter are these words:

> How great a gladness do you think the beauty of the flowers brought to his mind when he saw the shape of their beauty and perceived the odor of their sweetness? He used to turn the eye of consideration immediately to the beauty of that flower that comes from the root of Jesse and gives light in the days of spring and by its fragrance has raised innumerable thousands from the dead. When he found an abundance of flowers he preached to them and invited them to praise the Lord as though they were endowed with reason. In the same way he exhorted with the sincerest purity cornfields and vineyards, stones and forests and all the beautiful things of the fields, fountains of water and the green things of the gardens, earth and fire, air and wind, to love God and serve him willingly. Finally he called all creatures *brother*, and in a most extraordinary manner, a manner never experienced by others, he discerned the hidden things of nature with his sensitive heart, as one who had already escaped into the freedom of the glory of the sons of God ... for he was filled with love that surpasses all human understanding when he pronounced your holy name, O holy Lord; and carried away with joy and purest gladness, he seemed like a new man, one from another world.[4]

We shall be examining the mystical approach to the passion of Christ when we consider the stigmata, but even here there is an interweaving of nature and grace, of creation and redemption, and a sensitive, heart-felt awareness of his creatureliness and his participation in the interconnected web of creation.

It is not simply that Francis looked at creation as an objective observer, and taught moral lessons from the book of creation. Neither is it simply that he offered thanks for theological lessons learned about pattern, seasonal cycles, and mortality. Nor even that, like some of the schoolmen, he concocted philosophical arguments for the existence of God after the pattern of Anselm, Aquinas, or Descartes. Francis did not show interest in the God of the philosophers.

He actually entered into creation and discovered God in a mystical relation of love. This was not *pantheism*, in which the being of God resides in the natural order so that nature becomes God. We have learned a new word for an old experience — it is not the word *pantheism*, but *panentheism*. The being of God is not exhausted by creation, but rather dwells deep at the heart of things created, manifests his being and glory through them, so that they radiate and reflect something of his mysterious, transcendent, and unutterable glory.

Over the last two decades or so, we have rediscovered a more profound understanding of a spirituality of creation. It was always in the Bible, but had been forgotten in our theologies! I was fortunate because of the childhood inheritance I have spoken about, and was therefore 'inoculated' against the negative puritanism (Protestant and Catholic) that denied mystical experience. But now we are learning creation along with redemption, and rediscovering the glory that is Francis.

It may not be easy for us to recapture the organic relationship that Francis felt. I feel a profound gratitude to God for my own Celtic inheritance, and the intuitive rightness of organic images for living beings, so that I am shocked by mechanistic metaphors which are so pervasive in our secular language:

Until the industrial revolution occurred, in the minds of most people in the so-called 'developed' countries the dominant images were organic; they had to do with living things, they were biological, pastoral, agricultural or familial. God was seen as a 'shepherd', the faithful as 'the sheep of his pasture'. People who took care of the earth were said to practice 'husbandry'. Now we do not flinch to hear men and women referred to as 'units' as if they were machines. It is common, and considered acceptable, to refer to the mind as a 'computer', one's thoughts as 'inputs', other people's responses as feedback.[5]

135

As part of this package, we must ask such questions as: Can we simply trust the chemical industry as an altruistic benefactor in producing increasing amounts of drugs and fertilizers? Is the nuclear industry to be given *carte blanche* in supplying industrial and domestic power? Is the arms industry telling the truth in claiming to be the peacekeeper among the nations? Human sin, greed, and lust for power and money are the grim spectres which accompany these claims, and cause us to ask these questions.

Francis' organic relationship to the earth and all living beings is the key to our redemption and recovery in our polluted world. Bonaventure speaks of Francis' primeval innocence in his experience of a restored Eden, and indicates that the key to the problem of disharmony and sin is the compassion showed by Christ in his redemption:

> Compassion . . . is all-availing and it filled the heart of Francis and penetrated its depths to such an extent that his whole life seemed to be governed by it. It was loving compassion which united him to God in prayer and caused his transformation into Christ by sharing his sufferings. It was this which led him to devote himself humbly to his neighbour and enabled him to return to the state of primeval innocence by restoring man's harmony with the whole of creation.[6]

Questions of ecology and reconciliation mingle at this point, for the healing of the earth and its nations can only come from compassion, and from the divine compassion that Francis experienced in creation itself, and in the love of God revealed in Christ. It is at this point that we must turn to St Francis' *Canticle of Brother Sun*, which relates these themes in the context of adoration and praise.

God our Creator and Redeemer:
Your world manifests your wisdom, beauty and love,
  but we have disfigured it in ignorance, ugliness, and violence;
Have mercy upon us, Lord, and grant us a new awareness of our
  relatedness with the earth and with all living beings;
Give us the compassion of Jesus and the energy of the Holy
  Spirit, that the world may be renewed;
To the glory of your dear name. Amen.

14 ❧ *The Canticle of Brother Sun*

Il Cantico di Frate Sole[1]

1 Altissimo omnipotente bon Signore,
2 tue so le laude la gloria e l'onore e onne benedizione.

3 A te solo, Altissimo, se confano
4 e nullo omo è digno te mentovare.

5 Laudato sie, mi Signore, cun tutte le tue creature,
6 spezialmente messer lo frate Sole,
7 lo qual è iorno, e allumini noi per lui.

8 Ed ello è bello e radiante cun grande splendore:
9 de te, Altissimo, porta significazione.

10 Laudato si, mi Signore, per sora Luna e le Stelle:
11 im cielo l'hai formate clarite e preziose e belle.

12 Laudato si, mi Signore, per frate Vento,
13 e per Aere e Nubilo e Sereno e onne tempo
14 per lo quale a le tue creature dai sustentamento.

15 Laudato si, mi Signore, per sor Aqua,
16 la quale è molto utile e umile e preziosa e casta.

17 Laudato si, mi Signore, per frate Foco,
18 per lo quale enn' allumini la nocte:
19 ed ello è bello e iocundo e robustoso e forte.

20 Laudato si, mi Signore, per sora nostra matre Terra,
21 la quale ne sostenta e governa,
22 e produce diversi fructi con coloriti flori ed erba.

23 Laudato si, mi Signore, per quelli che perdonano per lo tuo amore
24 e sostengo infirmitate e tribulazione.

25 Beati quelli che 'l sosterrano in p̃ace,
26 ca da te, Altissimo, sirano incoranti.

27 Laudato si, mi Signore, per sora nostra Morte corporale,
28 de la quale nullo omo vivente po' scampare.

29 Guai a quelli che morrano ne le peccata mortali!
30 Beati quelli che trovarà ne le tue sanctissimi volantati,
31 ca la morte seconda no li farra male.

32 Laudate e benedicite mi Signore,
33 e rengraziate e serviteli cun grande umilitate.

The Canticle of Brother Sun[2]

1 Most high, all-powerful, all good, Lord!
2 All praise is yours, all glory, all honour and all blessing.

3 To you, alone, Most High, do they belong.
4 No mortal lips are worthy to pronounce your name.

5 All praise be yours, my Lord, through all that you have made,
6 And first my lord Brother Sun,
7 Who brings the day; and light you give to us through him.

8 How beautiful is he, how radiant in all his splendour!
9 Of you, Most High, he bears the likeness.

10 All praise be yours, my Lord, through Sister Moon and Stars;
11 In the heavens you have made them, bright and precious and fair.

12 All praise be yours, my Lord, through Brothers Wind and Air,
13 And fair and stormy, all the weather's moods,
14 By which you cherish all that you have made.

15 All praise be yours, my Lord, through Sister Water,
16 So useful, lowly, precious and pure.

17 All praise be yours, my Lord, through Brother Fire,
18 Through whom you brighten up the night.
19 How beautiful is he, how gay! Full of power and strength.

20 All praise be yours, my Lord, through Sister Earth, our mother,
21 Who feeds us in her sovereignty,
22 And produces various fruits with coloured flowers and herbs.

23 All praise be yours, my Lord, through those who grant pardon
24 For love of you; through those who endure sickness and trial.

25 Happy those who endure in peace,
26 By you, Most High, they will be crowned.

27 All praise be yours, my Lord, through Sister Death,
28 From whose embrace no mortal can escape.

29 Woe to those who die in mortal sin!
30 Happy those she finds doing your will!
31 The second death can do no harm to them.

32 Praise and bless my Lord, and give him thanks,
33 And serve him with great humility.

THE CANTICLE'S LEVELS OF MEANING

It is a mysterious and remarkable fact that Francis composed and sang his *Canticle* in the context of darkness, suffering and blindness, approaching the end of his earthly pilgrimage.

At La Verna he had received the seal of the stigmata upon his body, which indicated mystical union and identification with the crucified Jesus, and returning from the holy mountain he was brought to San Damiano.

The Church around him was filled with corruption, materialism, and crusading violence. His beloved Order of friars was invaded by schism, and there was wholesale departure from the simplicity and poverty of Francis' earlier vision. Humanly speaking, it could have led to self-pity and despair. But the darkest moment is just prior to dawn, so God's revelation of love and assurance was about to burst upon and within him.

In his utter weakness, Clare installed him in a hut next to the convent. 'For fifty days and more,' says the *Legend of Perugia*, 'blessed Francis could not bear the light of the sun during the day or the light of the fire at night. His eyes caused him so much pain that he could neither lie down nor sleep.'[3]

Beset by tribulations, with inward conflict and distress, he cried out in his agony that he might overcome the temptation of discouragement. Then suddenly, at the moment of his greatest need, God's voice came to him:

> 'Tell me, Brother: if, in compensation for your sufferings and tribulations you were given an immense and precious treasure: the whole mass of earth changed into pure gold, pebbles into precious stones, and the water of the rivers into perfume, would you not regard the pebbles and the waters as nothing compared to such a treasure? Would you not rejoice?' Blessed Francis answered: 'Lord, it would be a very great, very precious, and inestimable treasure beyond all that one can love and desire!' 'Well, Brother,' the voice said, 'be glad and joyful in the midst of your infirmities and tribulations: as of now, live in peace as if you were already sharing my kingdom.'[4]

As a direct result of this experience, Francis' darkness gave way to spiritual enlightenment, and he composed, out of his existential darkness, the beautiful hymn of light and glory, praising God in and through the wonders of creation.

A spirituality that can sustain a man or woman in such extremity, emerging victoriously through the refining fires of adversity and pain, is one that can only be explained by the reality of a suffering and compassionate God. Here there is a remarkable mingling of creation and redemption, for it is in this place, San Damiano, where Christ had first spoken to Francis from the crucifix twenty years before, that he now assures the stigmatized saint of his all-embracing love, and pours into him the joy of the Kingdom of God.

The redeemed soul often sings in the night, and the story of redemption is frequently expressed in images of creation that are symbols of interior and existential realities. St Paul relates the two in classic words:

> It is the God who said, 'Let light shine out of darkness,' who has shone in our hearts to give the light of the knowledge of the glory of God in the face of Jesus Christ.
> But we have this treasure in clay jars, so that it may be made clear that this extraordinary power belongs to God and does not come from us.[5]

We used to sing Francis' *Canticle* at Glasshampton Monastery every Sunday, and I could not help but relate the images of creation there to the experience of redemption, so when I discovered the Franciscan Eloi Leclerc's book *The Canticle of Creatures: Symbols of Union*, it simply confirmed what I had already intuited.

Leclerc's thesis is that the *Canticle* is not simply a celebration of matter praising the glory of the creator-God. The cosmic images of the external world are also symbolic of the inner realities of the soul or psyche. So when Francis writes and sings of sun, moon, stars, and creatures, he is naming realities of the unconscious, praising God through them, and experiencing God in them. It was when Leclerc read a paragraph by Paul Ricoeur that he found the key to interpreting the Canticle:

> To manifest the 'sacred' *on* the 'cosmos' and to manifest it *in* the 'psyche' are the same thing ... Cosmos and Psyche are the two poles of the same 'expressivity'; I express myself in expressing

the world; I explore my own sacrality in deciphering that of the world.[6]

In reading that statement, he saw in it the key to a reading of Francis' *Canticle* in terms of the interiority it reflects.

The *Canticle* is a poetical religious discourse on created things, but not simply that. They are the outward garment of a deeper kind of discourse. Praise of the cosmos is also the symbolic, unconsciously spoken language that expresses the interior journey of the depths of the soul. The illustration Leclerc uses is the story of the friars who were praying without Francis, at midnight, when suddenly a fiery solar chariot, surrounded by a great globe of light, filled the house:

> The watchers were dazed, and those who had been asleep were frightened; and they felt no less a lighting up of the heart than a lighting up of the body. Gathering together they began to ask one another what it was; but by the strength and grace of that great light each one's conscience was revealed to the others. Finally they understood and knew that it was the soul of their holy father that was shining with such great brilliance.[7]

Two things are happening here. Francis' love for creatures and love for God mingled in the clear, cosmic meaning of the text of the *Canticle*, and he entered into an ecstatic adoration of God in and through the created order. His whole life was a song, a dance, a prayer — an expression of the spiritual nature of the material world. The *Canticle* was a celebratory experience of all that. But also, beneath the surface and within the words, the sun, moon, and stars of the psyche radiate God's glory, and the wind, water, fire, and earth conjure up the profound movement of the Spirit in the depths of his being.

And that is not all. Francis portrays a man whose adoration and praise is expressed in the transcendence of God, and whose profound inward life is surrendered to the immanence of God.

In Leclerc's understanding, the *sun* represents a nature or cosmic mysticism, and the *cross* represents an evangelical mysticism. Francis therefore unites in his religious experience a union with God through the incarnation and cross of Christ — that is personal evangelical mysticism, *and* a fervent cosmic mysticism that recognizes the being and presence of the Spirit in the beauty and creatures of the world.

Leclerc marvels at such a uniting of the Sun and the cross, affirming that this synthesis resulted in one of the most profound and fascinating spiritual experiences any human being has ever had:

> The Canticle of Brother Sun is both praise of the cosmos and a hymn to the inner depths. When read according to its full meaning it proves to be the expression of the spiritual experience just described. What this brotherly praise of creatures, to the honour of the Most High, ultimately reveals to us is an approach to God that involves the saint simultaneously in a humble, fervent communion with all creatures and in the soul's opening of itself to its own innermost depths. Somewhat more precisely, it is an approach to God in which the soul, while communing in a humble brotherly way with creatures, is reconciled both to its entire self and to the entirety of reality.[8]

LIVING THE FRANCISCAN SYNTHESIS

These are the two images contained in the Franciscan synthesis — the Sun and the cross. The Sun represents Francis in relation to the created order — every creature is brother, sister, and mother within the maternal and paternal Fatherhood of God.

But Francis knows that we do not live in an Edenic paradise. Sin has invaded the world and its peoples, producing enmity, separation, and disintegration. The unity has been ruptured, humanity has fallen from grace and broken the covenant and heart of God.

Therefore the cross is indispensable in bridging the chasm caused by sin. God's broken heart has been revealed in his incarnation among his people. He has borne their griefs and carried their sorrows in the death and resurrection of Christ.

By way of the cross, the Sun rises again in the heart of the believer. The lost Eden is restored, and paradise regained. By this synthesis of Sun and cross a double blessing is experienced. Fallen humanity is reconciled to God, and the broken world is integrated again into a cosmic unity, so that the blessings of the future Kingdom are tasted now, and the powers of the world to come are already anticipated.

This sets the scene for the practical outworking of the synthesis. The Sun represents the ecological dimensions of our social and political lives. The cross represents the relational aspects of communal structures, national and international. In other words, a Franciscan spirituality commits the believer to cosmic renewal in all the tasks that go towards building a purified and renewed world on the one hand, and the work of forgiveness and reconciliation that builds up redeemed relationships throughout the world, on the other.

These are general statements, and the need is for increasing personal and communal networks and agencies through which particular tasks can be carried out.

It is not enough for us to sing songs of redemption and quote the poetry of nature. Like Francis, we have to repair the ruins with bricks and mortar, and we have to forgive and help our brothers and sisters with compassion and healing.

Both are necessary, and in a synthesis of Sun and cross we shall be able to set up common structures across religious and national barriers, to heal a disintegrated and polluted world. That is, if our Franciscan spirituality is genuine, and if we are serious about it.

FORGIVENESS AND RECONCILIATION

Lines 1–22 of the *Canticle* represent the cosmic stanzas in which Francis praises and experiences God in and through the creatures. Lines 23–31 contain two areas of human experience that were added later. The first concerns forgiveness and reconciliation between injured parties, and the second concerns our mortality, in which death is seen as our sister who carries us into the nearer presence of God.

Francis was a man of peace. He had found peace from the beginning of his conversion. It was peace *with* God through Jesus Christ his Saviour, and the peace *of* God flooding his inmost being. Because of that he became a messenger of peace and reconciliation, not only among the friars, sisters, and wider Franciscan communities, but among secular groups, authorities, and nations.[9]

Before he opened his mouth to preach, he prayed for peace, and then gave the greeting. Celano captures the moment:

> In all his preaching, before he proposed the word of God to those gathered about, he first prayed for peace for them, saying: 'The Lord give you peace.' He always most devoutly announced peace to men and women, to all he met and overtook. For this reason many who had hated peace and had hated also salvation embraced peace, through the cooperation of the Lord, with all their heart and were made children of peace and seekers after eternal salvation.[10]

Francis' inimitable way of making such an ideal practical is illustrated in his inspired intervention in the 'savage hatred' between the excommunicated mayor of Assisi, Podestà Berlingerio, and Bishop Guido of Assisi. Francis was very sick at the time, but in his distress at the quarrel he added a reconciliation strophe to his Canticle:

> All praise be yours, my Lord, through those who grant pardon
> For love of you; through those who endure sickness and trial.
>
> Happy those who endure in peace,
> By you, Most High, they will be crowned.

Then he sent Brother Pacifico to invite the podestà to the Bishop's Palace with the notables and others. Quite a crowd gathered, with great expectation and curiosity. Pacifico and his friar-musician told them of Francis' concern and love, and began to sing of the beauties of the world and the brothers and sisters of creation – composed by the blind saint. When they got to the stanzas of peace and forgiveness, something remarkable happened:

> The podestà stood up and joined his hands as for the gospel of the Lord, and he listened with great recollection and attention; soon tears flowed from his eyes, for he had a great deal of confidence in blessed Francis and devotion for him. At the end of the canticle, the podestà cried out before the entire gathering: 'In truth I say to you, not only do I forgive the lord bishop whom I ought to recognize as my master, but I would even pardon my brother's and my own son's murderer!' He then threw himself at the feet of the lord bishop and said to him: 'For the love of our Lord Jesus Christ and of blessed Francis, his servant, I am ready to make any atonement you wish.' The bishop stood up and said to him: 'My office demands humility of me, but by nature I am quick to anger; you must forgive me!' With much tenderness and affection, both locked arms and embraced each other.[11]

Francis was not a politician, and he put no trust in force of arms or secular political manoeuvring. But his gospel spoke not only of a personal evangelical experience, but of social justice and righteousness that is based on the compassion and love of God.

This means that contemporary Franciscans will have no *ultimate* hope in wordly political schemes to bring lasting peace – and this is only confirmed by the precarious relations among nations today.

Lasting peace comes only with the coming in glory of Jesus Christ to bring in his Kingdom. But if the follower of Francis, and therefore of Christ, is a person of peace, then there must be the *proximate* hope of peacemaking. Believing in the coming again of our Lord Jesus to establish his Kingdom of righteousness and peace does not absolve us from working through all legitimate political and social channels. If we are committed to the Prince of Peace, then we are committed to works of justice and peace and non-violent protest at injustice and inequality.

Engagement in violence has been a thorny problem in the Church ever since the so-called conversion of the emperor Constantine in the fourth century, when the Church moved from its early pacifism to an emerging doctrine of just war. But I cannot take any other position as a follower of Jesus, in the light of Francis, than that of pacifism and non-violent action in whatever ways are compatible with the gospel of reconciliation.

There are times when we can expect and experience remarkable manifestations of the grace and power of God in our peacemaking — and all our efforts must be undergirded with prayer and faith. But at all times, whether the presence of God is evident or seemingly absent, we must work together and with *all* men and women of good will, to promote peace and alleviate human and animal suffering at every level.

There are times when this may involve us in deprivation, risk, suffering, and even death. I remember being caught up short when I signed the Anglican Pacifist Fellowship/Fellowship of Reconciliation resolution that included words like the following: 'I protest the production and use of nuclear weapons, and do not wish myself or my family to be protected or defended by such means ...'

I am very conscious that it is not easy to take a pacifist stance in the world, or even in the Church. Things are not as black and white as they once appeared to me in those halcyon days of my early faith, when I stood in the dock of the Crown Court in Cardiff at seventeen years of age as a conscientious objector. There are many loose ends in my pacifism, but when the chips are down, and in the face of violence that always begets further violence, I have to say: 'Here I stand; I can do no other.'[12] But my Franciscan heart sings when I read the story of light and darkness with which I conclude this chapter.

It comes right at the end of Eloi Leclerc's book on the *Canticle* that has given us much of the substance of this chapter. The book sparkles with theological and psychological awareness, and is an example of remarkable Franciscan scholarship. Leclerc argues and applies his thesis in a scholarly and intuitive manner, and concludes the volume with an Epilogue that is both startling and sadly beautiful.

It begins: 'April 1945: The Allied armies are penetrating deep into the heart of Germany.' Then he goes on to describe the journey of a Nazi freight train from Passau to Munich, loaded with thousands of French and other prisoners, packed like sardines into carriages, shut in for twenty-one days. Hundreds had died, hundreds were dying, delirious from hunger and beaten into submission. Leclerc was among them, and he describes the horror of living skeletons, of bestial cruelty, of human degradation perpetrated by the SS guards — and five sons of Francis among them.[13]

> The dead! There are more and more of them. Many of our comrades die of dysentery; many of exhaustion. Others have contracted erysipelas and are the most horrible spectacle of all. Within a night or a day, these men become unrecognizable; their swollen fiery faces are completely distorted. Delirious with fever, these unfortunates fill the night with their yelling; they scream for water, but in vain. In the morning their bodies lie stiff in death. Sometimes the corpses remain in the car throughout the day, washed by the pools of water that have formed on the flooring.

At last it is clear that one of the five friars is about to breathe his last, and Leclerc speaks of the absence of the Father in the Son's agony of soul, sorrowful unto death:

> Black night fills our souls. And yet, on the morning of April 26 when one of us is in his last moments and the light has almost left his eyes, what rises from our hearts to our lips is not a cry of despair or rebellion, but a song, a song of praise: Francis of Assisi's *Canticle of Brother Sun*! Nor do we have to force ourselves to sing it. It rises spontaneously out of our darkness and nakedness, as though it were the only language fit for such a moment.

There was no flight of larks overhead, he says, but a supernatural peace filled their hearts. That evening, they carried his body for burial, accompanied by blows from the SS because they were not quick enough. Leclerc concludes the Epilogue by saying: 'How could we forget such an experience when we read today Francis of Assisi's *Canticle of Brother Sun*?'

Blessèd Lord:
Francis entered into the joy and mystery of created things,
And in them discerned the life of your Holy Spirit;
He sang of their glory and of peace and reconciliation
    among humankind.
Enable us to see your glory in the brothers and sisters of
    the created order,
To love and forgive the whole human family, and to become
    instruments of your peace;
Through Jesus Christ our Lord. Amen.

15 ❧ *Sister Bodily Death*

THE ULTIMATE POVERTY

Francis was naked when he was born into this world. He stripped himself naked before his father and the crowd at twenty-four years of age when he embraced the poverty and renunciation of his vocation. And at last he asked to be laid on the ground naked as a preparation for his death in 1226.

I remember, just before I left Glasshampton Monastery to explore the hermit life, my experience at the death of one of our older friars. The brother died at night. The doctor had left, and I was left alone to lay out the body and perform the last offices.

At one point I looked at the naked body, thin but not emaciated, which represented all that was left in the world of the physical and material part of this friar, for his possessions were few and financially valueless.

His dying had been easy at the last, and there was something beautiful about the naked body, the silent hour of the night in the monastery, and the final stripping, praying, and commending of his soul to God by the light of the sanctuary light that burned at his side through the rest of the night. A real Franciscan death.

The amazing thing about a Franciscan understanding of death, which springs directly from the dying experience of Francis, is that there is a welcoming, friendly relationship — as if it were all of a pattern. We are well used to thinking of death as the enemy, the wages of sin, the grim reaper, the antithesis of life. There is truth in all that, of course. It is the shadow side of death, beset with fears and tinged with terrors.

But there is also the blessedness of death as rest from labour, handmaid of the Lord, entry into life, portal of eternity — Sister Death. It has its part in the interrelated and cosmic web and pattern of the cosmos, participating in the cycle of the seasons, mortality and finitude giving way to a blessèd dying which is in the natural order of things.

So when his last sickness was upon him, in all his pain, vomiting, and weariness, Francis got his brothers to sing for him the *Canticle* that he had composed at San Damiano. So near to death, yet surrounded by singing and adoration, Brother Elias was scandalized, even though Francis was comforted and rejoicing.

He remonstrated with Francis, saying that the people of Assisi venerated him as a saint, knowing he was dying of an incurable disease, and they would be perplexed at the sound of praises sung by day and night. They would say: 'How can this man show so much joy when he is about to die? He ought to be preparing himself for death.'

Through his pain, Francis turned to Elias in great fervour of spirit, and said: 'Brother, allow me in my infirmities to rejoice in the Lord and in His praises, for by the grace and assistance of the Holy Spirit I am so united and conjoined by my Lord that by His mercy I may rightly rejoice in Him, the Most High.'[1]

The *Speculum*, which reports this incident, is anxious to share another precious moment that reveals Francis' attitude to his death and that encapsulates in wonderful words the positive Franciscan affirmation of joy in the face of the last enemy who has been transformed into a dear friend.

It concerns the visit of a friendly doctor, John Buono, from Arrezzo. Francis asked him: 'What do you think about this dropsical disease of mine?' 'Brother,' said the doctor, 'God willing, all will be well with you.'

But Francis would not be fobbed off with evasion. 'Tell me the truth,' he persisted. 'Don't be afraid to tell me, for by God's grace I am not such a coward as to fear death. By the grace and help of the Holy Spirit I am so united to my Lord that I am equally content to die or to live.'

The doctor then told him frankly: 'Father, according to our medical knowledge your disease is incurable, and it is my belief that you will die either at the end of September or in early October.'

Then blessed Francis, says the *Speculum*, lying on his bed, most reverently and devoutly stretched out his hands to God, and with great joy of mind and body, said: 'Welcome, Sister Death.'[2]

A PATTERN FOR DYING

If we follow our Lord in the way of St Francis, perhaps we should read again the primary sources of his dying. The period really lasted two years, from the time he received the wounds of Jesus in his body at La Verna in 1224, up to his lying naked on the ground, asking Angelo and Leo to sing to him of Sister Death in 1226.[3]

There is such a thing as dying grace, but no one can boast of it, or be glib about it, who has not walked in that valley of the shadow. I have shared with many, both medically and as a priest and friar, who have travelled that path and through the gateway of death. But I have not yet been that way myself.

Six months before writing this chapter, one night, alone and in the darkness of my hermitage, I was suddenly attacked by a fearful swinging vertigo, palpitations, hot and cold sweating, which lasted intermittently through the night. Well do I remember keeling over at 4.15 a.m. when I tried to stand, and then getting on my prayer-stool, able to keep some kind of balance as long as I held myself upright.

I kept in my mind the experiences of some of the terminally ill people for whom I had been praying during that period, and found grace and help in the *Jesus Prayer* until the hours of daylight came and eventually I was able to find medical help.

Since then the symptoms have abated and I am making the journey back to balance and normality again, under supervision. This week, during my prayers, I found myself reading, with great wonder and admiration, the hymn of the saintly Richard Baxter, expressing similar sentiments to those of Francis:

> Lord, it belongs not to my care
>   Whether I die or live:
> To love and serve you is my share,
>   And this your grace must give.
>
> Christ leads me through no darker rooms
>   Than he went through before;
> He that into God's kingdom comes
>   Must enter by this door.
>
> My knowledge of that life is small,
>   The eye of faith is dim;
> But 'tis enough that Christ knows all,
>   And I shall be with him.

Suppose you or I should hear from our physician the words that Francis heard from John Buono. What would our attitude be? That of St Francis and Richard Baxter? John Wesley said of the early Methodists: 'Our people die well.'

The first Franciscans reflect the attitude of the early Church under persecution. To live for Christ was glorious – to die for him was even better.

When Francis was at Acre in 1219, he learned that five of his friars had shed their blood in martyrdom in Morocco after being flogged and drenched in burning oil. 'Now I can flatter myself of having indeed five Friars Minor,' he cried. Francis himself desired martyrdom, and he could quite easily have said the words uttered by Cyprian, Bishop of Carthage, who was martyred in the Valerian persecution of the first century:

> Earth is shut against us, but heaven is opened; death overtakes us, but immortality follows; the world recedes, but Paradise receives. What honour, what peace, what joy, to shut our eyes on the world and men, and open them on the face of God and His Christ! Oh, short and blessed voyage.[4]

At this point we see that Francis' welcoming of Sister Death is of a piece with the whole *Canticle*. He is not rejoicing that his poor body is to be set free from its mortality, or that this is the end of his suffering.

Rather, he is 'letting go' his narrow individuality in order to embrace the fullness of being in God. For eternity is not simply a continuity of our egocentric individuality, but an entering into the communion of saints and into the fullness of God's eternal Being.

He cannot any longer enjoy for himself the sun, moon, stars, and fire of the *Canticle*. But in and through them he praises the eternal and creative splendour of God, in whose greater fullness Francis is from henceforth going to consummate his existence.

Eloi Leclerc understands the *Canticle* as the expression of truly radical conversion. There is a letting go of limited, conscious individuality in embracing death, and a growing concern with all that has to do with God's Being in its fullness. The existential centre of gravity has been displaced:

> The man who has thus put himself into the hands of Being now sees everything, including death, in the positive light of Being. Death is for him no longer the alien destroyer; she is that only to a man who clings to his ego. 'Woe to those who die in mortal sin,' says Francis immediately after greeting Sister Death. Mortal sin, sin that brings death to the soul, is precisely the closing in of the conscious self upon itself and its individuality; it is self-possession at any price, a protective withdrawal into the self that turns being into having.[5]

Francis himself describes the deathbed of a grasping, egocentric man who, even as he faces the grim necessity of death, shrinks into his clinging self and cannot let go. 'All the talent and ability, all the learning and wisdom which he thought his own, are taken away from him.' Such a death, says Francis, causes 'such anguish and distress that only a person who has experienced it can appreciate it'.[6]

The wretchedness of such a man exemplifies the degeneration of a person who was meant for transformation. This man that Francis describes was eager for religion, but he could not let go his possessions. He even conceived of immortality as a coveted possession, and instead of attaining to fullness of being in God (what the Bible calls eternal life), his being disintegrated into the hell of non-being.

I greatly appreciate the poetry and prose of Dylan Thomas, but there is one poem of his which makes me very sad, and is the antithesis of St Francis welcoming death as sister, and a gateway into the wider, deeper, fellowship of life and love. It is the poem 'Do not go gentle into that good night',[7] and comes from 1941, when Dylan's father was dying.

The anguish of the poem evokes more of the poet's dilemma than his father's pain, calling upon the dying man to rave, rage, and curse as life's day dies and the darkness of death overtakes him. The whole feeling of the poem, tortured with grief and fear, reveals a particularly western and secular attitude of one who has lost his profound Celtic inheritance in which finitude and mortality are caught up into the dimension of faith and mystery.

NEW MORAL QUESTIONS CONCERNING DEATH

Part of the Franciscan attitude is reverence for life and prayer for a good death. Part of the new questioning concerns abortion on demand, soaring suicide rates, legalizing of euthanasia, and the fearful technological apparatus for keeping people alive when they should have been allowed to die.

These are contemporary problems that face a society that sees no need for God, and soon it sees no need for reverence for the unborn child, tenderness for the sick and elderly, care for the terminally ill, and the preparation and sustaining of a person towards a good death.

I am not writing against the 'good humanist' in saying these things, for often he or she has sympathy for the Franciscan attitude. I am speaking of those who have opted for a hedonistic life-style, money, ambition, power, and influence – in pursuit of which they have neglected their true selves and ignored the profound and mysterious call of God within.

Over the last decade, within our Franciscan houses, there has been an ongoing dialogue about our ministry and responsibility to our ageing and dying friars and sisters, and this has also spread to the Third Order.

In our wider society, urgent questions have been raised because of nuclear families who have no room to nurse sick and aged parents, and Britain is following America in questions of nursing the sick from an emptying purse. A paragraph from my weekly newspaper voices the problem from the American side of the Atlantic:

One of our friends has, in her hands a hospital bill, some 70 pages long and $200,000 insurance dollars deep for her brother's last month of what barely qualified as life. Another colleague is trying to tally up, just for the macabre curiosity, what Medicare paid for her husband's last days: the cost of coma.[8]

The article goes on to say that the 'full medical regalia' — tubes and respirators galore — like some horrifying fireworks display of *What Medicine Can Do, Circa 1993*, was not wanted. And the further problem is that it is the accountant who is the spectre standing behind the physician, deciding who lives and who dies. These fears are compounded by the survey of doctors and nurses who treat dying patients, which speaks of the worry that they give too much treatment and too little pain relief.

Even with good medical intentions, there may occur the sad scenario described by Dr Maurice Rawlings:

I remember one elderly patient who existed in a depressed atmosphere in a rather repugnant nursing home. A forgotten patient among other deprived souls he was treated as a protoplasmic nonentity. One day he became acutely ill with pneumonia, was transferred to the nearest hospital where antibiotics, oxygen, and intravenous medications were to no avail. Although medical treatment was good, he died. He had received no treatment of the emotions and no care for the soul. He was friendless, frightened, forgotten, and alone. There was no opportunity for him to talk to anyone about finance, family, religion or death. And no one asked him if he was prepared for life after death.[9]

155

In the face of all this, there is much that can be done. At a professional level, much research and dialogue is taking place, illustrated by the enlightened approach of Dr Elisabeth Kübler-Ross with medical students on the care of the dying.

In her book *On Death and Dying*, she evaluates the psychological stages through which the terminally ill may pass when they, and their loved ones, are told of their condition. This is the result of work with more than two hundred patients, and she lists these experienced stages as: denial, anger, bargaining, depression, acceptance.[10]

Then there is the work of the hospice movement, with its sterling work for the terminally ill and dying, and the relief of patients in the assurance that their pain can and will be controlled. It was Dr Cicely Saunders who founded the St Christopher Hospice for the dying in 1967, and this has since taken off into an expression of the deepest concern for patients and their families, enabling them to face death not only with acceptance, but in faith and hope. Her moving collection of meditations for the suffering and bereaved, *Beyond All Pain*, is a radiant witness to the hospice movement.[11]

THE ETERNAL DIMENSION

A contemporary Franciscan spirituality must be rooted firmly in the soil of this world, leading the way in the application of gospel values of compassion, justice, and peace in a war-torn and violent society. But there must be no neglect of the transcendent dimension of faith — a full-blooded affirmation and following of Christ in all his fullness. And this includes the dimension of eternity.

There is no doubt, in the Franciscan story, that there is the expectation of a fuller life in God after death. We have seen that there are new moral and theological problems which have to do with birth, life, and death at the end of the twentieth century; so also there is a new interest in death itself and the implications of life beyond the present horizons.

During the 1960s and 1970s, it became possible and then fashionable to talk about sexuality at all levels while still keeping death in the closet. During the 1980s and 1990s, the taboos around the subject of death have been, and are, lifted.

The catholic or evangelical believer, and certainly the Franciscan, does not look for proofs of survival in terms of *post-mortem* evidence; but if respectable scientific and pastoral research is present, we ought not to neglect it.

Research in the area of terminal illness, and modern resuscitation methods, have brought to light evidence of survival beyond clinical death. I must show caution here, for I am not indicating objective, scientific proof of survival after death, but important medically recorded experiences of persons who have 'died' and undergone resuscitation.

The old definition of clinical death, viz. cessation of respiration and heart-beat, has given way to a new definition of brain death. It is with those who have been brought back through cardio-pulmonary resuscitation (CPR) with whom I am concerned here — the 'near-death experience'.

For those who want to read up the evidence, the writings of Dr Elisabeth Kübler-Ross, Dr Raymond Moody, and others should be perused — physicians of high standing with no theological axe to grind.[12]

I am not seeking to support or buttress theological considerations, but pointing to clear and objective evidence from unbiased and reputable medical and psychiatric practitioners. The point is that through CPR techniques an increasing number of people have been resuscitated who previously would not have survived. The technique is now in widespread use in medical, first-aid, and industrial practice, and is continually giving rise to greater interest from every quarter.

Dr Raymond Moody's first book, *Life after Life*, has the sub-title *The Investigation of a Phenomenon — Survival of Bodily Death*. Dr Kübler-Ross writes in the Foreword that it is evident 'that the dying patient continues to have a conscious awareness of his environment after being pronounced clinically dead'. What she read in Moody's researches confirmed her own findings.

Moody himself says: 'I am now uncovering new cases of this phenomenon so rapidly that I am no longer keeping track of the exact number.' He goes on to affirm that, on the basis of research work among physicians and surgeons, the question will soon not be *whether* there is really such a phenomenon, but rather what are we to make of it.

This is not the place to review the evidence of case histories, but it is worth reproducing the theoretically complete 'model experience' that Moody constructs on the basis of his research.

It embodies all the *common* elements of typical near-death experiences:

> A man is dying and, as he reaches the point of greatest physical distress, he hears himself pronounced dead by his doctor. He begins to hear an uncomfortable noise, a loud ringing or buzzing, and at the same time feels himself moving very rapidly through a long tunnel. After this he suddenly finds himself outside of his own physical body, but still in the immediate physical environment, and he sees his own body from a distance, as though he is a spectator. He watches the resuscitation attempt from this unusual vantage point and is in a state of emotional upheaval.
>
> After a while, he collects himself and becomes more accustomed to his odd condition. He notices that he still has a 'body', but one of a very different nature and with very different powers from the physical body he has left behind. Soon other things begin to happen. Others come to meet and to help him. He glimpses the spirits of relatives and friends who have already died, and a loving, warm spirit of a kind he has never encountered before − a being of light − appears before him. This being asks him a question, non-verbally, to make him evaluate his life and helps him along by showing him a panoramic, instantaneous playback of the major events in his life. At some point he finds himself approaching some sort of barrier or border, apparently representing the limit between earthly life and the next life. Yet he finds that he must go back to the earth, that the time for his death has not yet come. At this point he resists, for by now he is taken up with his experiences in the afterlife and does not want to return. He is overwhelmed by intense feelings of joy, love and peace. Despite his attitude, though, he somehow reunites with his physical body and lives.
>
> Later he tries to tell others, but he has trouble doing so. In the first place, he can find no human words adequate to describe these unearthly episodes. He also finds that others scoff, so he stops telling other people. Still, the experience affects his life profoundly, especially his views about death and its relationship to life.[13]

If you want the personal and experiential detail, you have to go to the personal case histories, which yield a great deal of beauty and intuitive wisdom. The light is not blinding, but soft and radiant; there is a network of thought-communication, a heightened sense of perception, and the awareness of peace, ease, and quietness. There is the removal of fear, and the anticipation of meeting loved ones, with the manifestation of the 'personal being of light'.

Before such research was reported publicly, there was reticence about sharing these experiences, but members of the medical profession themselves, as a result of their research, are coming to affirm survival after death. As Moody says of himself: 'I have come to accept as a matter of religious faith that there is a life after death, and I believe that the phenomenon we have been examining is a manifestation of that life.'

I am not interested in marshalling evidence to convince others of human survival, but it would be stupid to ignore what seems to be genuine evidence based on careful research. Much of it is independent evidence, as it comes from outside the specifically Christian tradition, but it is supportive of what we accept as part of our faith. This is certainly true of our Franciscan sources, for the life of Francis and his brothers and sisters is full of the interwoven network of this life and the life to come.

From among the stories of Francis' 'out of the body' and post-death appearances one is reported by Celano. At a Chapter meeting in Florence, Brother Anthony was preaching with great fervour on the text 'Jesus of Nazareth, King of the Jews' when Brother Monaldo looked towards the door and saw Francis raised up into the air, his arms extended as though on a cross, blessing the brothers. The effect of this appearance was that the joy and consolation of the Holy Spirit filled the whole Chapter.[14]

The Franciscan witness is not simply one of survival, but of joy, consummation, a new place of existence, a new dimension of growth and maturity in God, no longer hampered by finitude and mortality, but vibrant with resurrection life in a new body of immortality. This is the context in which the *Speculum* ends the story of Francis, on the borderland of heaven:

> ... after twenty years of perfect penitence, he departed to the Lord Jesus Christ, Whom he had loved with all his heart, with all his mind, with all his soul, and all his strength, with the most ardent desire and with utter devotion, following Him perfectly, hastening swiftly in His footsteps, and at last coming in the greatest glory to Him Who lives and reigns with the Father and the Holy Spirit for ever and ever. *Amen*.[15]

LIVING IN THE LIGHT OF ETERNITY

This chapter has turned our minds to the experience we shall all undergo sooner or later. Franciscan spirituality embraces our present mortality and the strong hope of that eternal life which begins in this life and enters its fullness after our earthly journey. How can we live in this awareness, allowing the hope of glory to shine on our daily lives? Here are some suggestions:

1 Set aside some study and prayer time to think and pray about Christian teaching on death and eternal life, reflecting on your own mortality and praying for a good death.

2 Interest yourself in the hospice movement at some level. Not everyone is suited to it, but ask the Lord if you should visit or help in some way in its work.

3 Look around your neighbourhood and see if there is anything you can do, individually or as a family, for the chronically/terminally ill, or recently bereaved neighbours.

4 In view of the increasing financial demands on the Health Service, can you share in the new social vision and concern for elderly people in their last years?

5 If you belong to a Franciscan meeting/Third Order, and there was the possibility of such a group living communally, taking in one or two terminally ill people, how would you respond to some share in that?

6 Do you regularly pray for your departed friends and loved ones? Have you thought of the meaning of *All Saints' Day* and *All Souls' Day,* and a requiem Eucharist for those who die with no one to remember them?

Lord Jesus Christ:
You are our Saviour who was dead, but who now lives forever,
possessing the keys of hell and of death;
Remove from us, we pray, all fear of death, and enable us,
like our father Francis, to embrace our death as sister
and friend when our time comes;
Until then, grant us a ministry to the dying, and faithfulness
in prayer and love for the departed;
For you are our resurrection and our life. Amen.

16 🌿 Mystical Life

WHAT IS MYSTICISM?

Before we talk about the mystical life of St Francis, we need to say something about mysticism generally. As a teenage Christian, my teaching at church came from a Protestant and Reformed source, but my secret reading was found in the Catholic mystical tradition. My copies of *Brother Lawrence* and *St John of the Cross* were under brown-paper covers!

It was not confined to Christian mysticism, for wherever I found the word it led to descriptive writing and experience that was fascinating. If you want to dip your toe into that immense ocean of mind-blowing universal experience that may be subsumed under the name mysticism, I commend the study and anthology compiled by F. C. Happold in his book *Mysticism*, for it is too wide and deep to undertake here. Happold will introduce you to many traditions, writers, and mystics. His writings have been a treasure-trove to me, and never fail to stimulate and enthuse me every time I turn to them. The other book for which I would sell my shirt is *The Oxford Book of English Mystical Verse* – out of print now, but if you find a second-hand copy blessèd are you!

The word mysticism may be used in a loose manner in speaking of a universal experience of immediacy and intuition, or it may be used in a disciplined description of religious experience. The particular mystical element is that of religious *feeling* and certainty. Although it is not anti-rational, it gives primacy to the emotional life in the forming of an intellectual attitude. Think of St Francis alongside this description of a mystic:

> In the true mystic there is an extension of normal consciousness, a release of latent powers and a widening of vision, so that aspects of truth unplumbed by the rational intellect are revealed to him. Both in feeling and thought he apprehends an immanence of the temporal in the eternal and the eternal in the temporal. In the religious mystic there is a direct experience of the Presence of God. Though he may not be able to describe it in words, though he may not be able logically to demonstrate its validity, to the mystic his experience is fully and absolutely valid and is surrounded with complete certainty. He has been 'there', he has 'seen', he 'knows'. With St Paul, in the poem by F. W. H. Myers, he can say:
>
>> Whoso has felt the spirit of the Highest
>> Cannot confound nor doubt Him nor deny.
>> Yea with one voice, O world, though thou deniest,
>> Stand thou on that side, for on this am I.[1]

Now let me clarify my definition a little more. In my reading, I encountered what seemed to be three categories of mysticism that answered to my experience. There is a certain overlapping, but they looked like this:

Nature mysticism

For me, this welled up from my childhood relationship with that in nature which was mysterious — a kind of reciprocal awareness of earth, sea, and sky. This was part of my Celtic heritage, and pagan in the neutral (and good) sense. I intuited it before I read it! It is universal, of course, and I soon came across it in the poetry of Shelley and Wordsworth, and in that beautiful, melancholy account of Richard Jeffries' search, *The Story of My Heart*. Henry Vaughan, like Wordsworth, laments its loss when leaving childhood:

> And looking back — at that short space —
> Could see a glimpse of His Bright Face:
> When on some gilded cloud, or flow'r,
> My gazing soul would dwell an hour,
> And in those weaker glories spy
> Some shadows of eternity:
> Before I taught my tongue to wound
> My Conscience with a sinful sound,
> Or had the black art to dispense
> A several sin to ev'ry sense,
> But felt through all this fleshly dress
> Bright shoots of everlastingness.

I never lost it. Even now I am arrested, overwhelmed, and sometimes ecstatic in unexpected moments of sheer cosmic glory.

Person mysticism

This is sometimes called *soul mysticism*, for it has to do with the profound depth of one's own being, and that of the reciprocal relationship with others. I was both gregarious and a lover of solitude. In relationships, I found I could relate in joyous sharing, emotional depth, and sympathetic sorrow with boys and girls, men and women — and other creatures too.

This welled up from the depths of my own heart, and I remember a joyful recognition of it in Martin Buber's *I and Thou*, and the stories of the way in which Buber related in mystical depth and union of heart with people and creation.

Soul mysticism has much to do with a profound discovery of the numinous and hidden depths of oneself. As a child, I found myself wondering about *who* I was, *what* I was, *how* I was — and my solitude was part of that search. But another part of it was to find myself in others, to reach out in yearning relationships, to discover my own soul in the other, and to enable him or her to discover themselves in me.

God mysticism

It is difficult to separate this category from the former two, because that mystery which stirred my depths in the cosmos and confronted me in the yearning of human relationships was in continuity with the immanence of God. In God mysticism, the soul is not satisfied with intuiting, yearning, and discovering. There is an inward drive towards union — the return of the spirit to its immortal Ground, its infinite Source.

In the Christian mystical tradition, there is no loss, but an enhancement of individuality in the fuller and deeper communion with and in God. It is a process of deification and union, a participation in the very life of God. The term *theosis* or *divinization* is used in the Eastern Church.

Franciscan mysticism and the Gospel

Now I want to show that as this threefold understanding was part of my own experience, so it can be seen in the life of Francis, and is part of the biblical and gospel tradition.

Nature mysticism is reflected in many parts of the Old Testament, and especially in some of the nature psalms, where the mystery of God's inspiration breathes through all creatures:

> When you hide your face, they
>   are dismayed;
>   when you take away their
>   breath, they die
>   and return to their dust.
> When you send forth your
>   spirit, they are created;
>   and you renew the face of the
>   ground.[2]

In the New Testament, there is a mystical sense of the God of creation becoming incarnate by the Spirit, in order to bring about the redemption and reconciliation of the fallen cosmic order.

The God of creation and the God of redemption is inextricably united in the sheer theological beauty and symmetry of the eighth chaper of Paul's letter to the Romans. The Greek verb *stenazo* is used three times, bearing the meaning *to sigh, groan,* or *give vent* to deep feelings of yearning, aspiration, or anxiety. It is associated, too, with the travail of labour in childbirth as an analogy for creative prayer. The threefold repetition of the word (vv. 22, 23, 26) with its maternal overtones is intimately connected with the feminine *ruach* or *Spirit* of God, moving and breathing over the confusion of the primeval chaos, begetting form, order, and life.

The point I am making here is that the same word *stenazo* (*groaning*) depicts the mystical travail of creation itself, of the believer's yearning for fullness, and of the Spirit of God within both:

> *Verse 22:* We know that the whole creation has been *groaning* in labor pains until now ...
>
> *Verse 23:* ... and not only the creation, but we ourselves, who have the first fruits of the Spirit, *groan* inwardly while we wait for adoption, the redemption of our bodies.
>
> *Verse 26:* Likewise the Spirit helps us in our weakness; for we do not know how to pray as we ought, but that very Spirit intercedes with sighs too deep for words [i.e., *groanings* unutterable].

This is a cosmic mysticism of universal proportions, biblical and Franciscan in its embrace. It expresses the universal groaning of the Holy Spirit, crying, sighing, and yearning beyond all description, knowing, or imagining. These are the unutterable groanings which arise from *Ruach Yahweh*, the Spirit of God, whose breathing pervades the whole cosmos.

Now I want to apply to the life of Francis these three categories of nature mysticism, person mysticism, and God mysticism, linking them with the threefold way of Christian mysticism, as Bonaventure did in his biography of Francis, and in his *Tree of Life* and *The Soul's Journey Into God.*

THE MYSTIC WAY:
PURGATION, ILLUMINATION, AND UNION

These stages on the mystic way are rooted in universal human experience, though their use to denote the pattern of mystical prayer comes from the sixth century writings of a Syrian monk known as pseudo-Dionysius the Areopagite.[3]

Francis never laid down any systematic 'Way to God' or any kind of didactic spirituality. His was an intuitive, spontaneous and inebriated way of living out the grace of God and the energies of the Spirit. Nevertheless, he was a man of great discipline and orthodoxy.

Bonaventure, in the next generation, though completely enthralled by Francis, was a systematician and organizer, as well as a profoundly spiritual friar. In his *Life of Francis*, he pointed up the classic mystic way, lived out in all its profundity and glory. It may be set out like this:

Chapters 1–4:   Francis' early life, conversion, foundation, and spread of the Order.

Chapters 5–7:   PURGATION: The threefold vow, austerity of life, humility, obedience, and poverty.

Chapters 8–10:   ILLUMINATION: Francis' affectionate holiness, brotherly relation to all creatures, his fervour, compassion, and desire for martyrdom for Christ, his zeal for, and power in, prayer.

Chapters 11–13:   UNION (or Perfection): Loyalty and understanding of Scripture, power and inspiration in preaching, gifts of healing and discernment, increasing sanctification, culminating in the sacred stigmata.

Chapters 13–15:   From the stigmata, deepening holiness and awareness of God towards his death and canonization.[4]

This threefold classification is useful, but should not be pressed too strictly, for sometimes the mystic way is more like a slope than a staircase. Nevertheless, it is useful to think of it as a spiral staircase in which the stages 'come around again' at a different level as the ascending staircase retraces itself. So the stages are not successive, so much as concurrent, and there is constant overlap.

I shall apply these stages to Francis' experience, but it is well to note their universality in terms of any serious discipline. I went for a walk with one of our postulants who was an accomplished organist. He talked to me about his approach to learning one of J. S. Bach's *Prelude and Fugue* studies.

First, he would take the music manuscript and study it in his hands, to get the feel and sense of the composition. Then, when he was ready, he would begin, repetitively and painfully, to play what was before him. This was followed by a second stage of enlightenment, glimpsing the aim and style of the composer, seeing into the inwardness of the music, and being caught up momentarily into the glory and greatness of the interpretation. Then came the gradual movement into the stage of what might be called union — the surrender of eyes and ears, hands, feet and soul, on the keys, pedals, stops, and pipes of the organ, until there was a blending of mind, heart, and body in union with the genius of the great Bach.

One can see the pattern of *purgation, illumination,* and *union* here, and it may be applied to any of the great disciplines of art or science, for it is a pattern of application, practice, progress, and maturity.

As a reflection of the gospel, *purgation* answers to the conviction of sin, baptism of repentance, and a stripping of the old self of sin, pride, and egocentricity; *illumination* answers to forgiveness, flashes of enlightenment and joy, and the sacramental food of Christian pilgrimage; *union* is the increasing experience of participation in the life of God, until one passes from shadow into reality, consummated in union with God in the divine life of heaven.

If we examine Francis' pilgrimage in the light of these stages, it becomes clear that it was a mystical journey, combining a creation spirituality and a redemption spirituality, culminating in identification with Christ in the stigmata upon Mount La Verna.

Purgation

The pattern for Francis, as for us all, is to follow in the footsteps of Christ, and the key scripture is found in Hebrews 12.1–2:

> Let us . . . lay aside every weight and the sin that clings so closely, and let us run with perseverance the race that is set before us, looking to Jesus the pioneer and perfecter of our faith, who for the sake of the joy that was set before him endured the cross, disregarding its shame, and has taken his seat at the right hand of the throne of God.

Purgation is the process which begins when the soul first realizes the need of God, often accompanied by world-weariness or disillusion. It involves repentance and purification from sin, leading to all the positive blessings of the gospel.

In Francis' experience, this process probably began when he was imprisoned in Perugia at twenty years of age, cut off from the sun, sea, and sky, which led to his later fever and loss of vitality and joy as he looked over the plain of Umbria in his convalescence.

It was also a cathartic experience for Francis to become disillusioned with his knightly ambitions when he heard the voice in Spoleto telling him to renounce the proposed military vocation for the sake of the greater Lord. And a further step in the purgative process was taken when he saw and smelt the putrifying sores of the leper on the road. He purposely embraced him — a mortifying experience if ever there was one. Celano indicates that the leper was Christ.[5]

Repairing the churches around Assisi, beginning with San Damiano, was also part of the same process, for this involved humility, discipline, courage, and perseverance, with a stripping away of pride and self-will.

It is no coincidence that 'stripping' was a very literal description of what happened when Francis underwent that purgative experience of shedding all his clothes and walking away from his father and the crowd in utter nakedness at the beginning of his life of poverty, in 1206.

In his teaching and example to the friars, Francis showed himself particularly aware of the sophisticated and evasive complications by which we sinners avoid radical confrontation with the holiness of God. He would smell out insincerity and hypocrisy in pseudo-hermits who kept silence because they didn't want to be found out, in friars-to-be who were inflated with their own egocentric desires, or in friars who were lazy and gluttonous, whom he sent on their way.[6]

In this purging or pruning, there is certain to be searing pain involved, and most of us shrink from it and evade facing the surgery. But the next tribulation, catastrophic illness, bereavement, or circumstance throws us on to God in complete helplessness, so that he uses even these things to lead us from purgation into illumination.

Yet there is also joy in repentance, and the New Testament word for it is *metanoia*, which means to 'change your heart' rather than 'do penance'. God is not an irritable old man in the sky, hurling thunderbolts of despotic anger on to the earth, nor an exacting tyrant who demands retribution. He is rather the yearning father who rejoices when his son or daughter returns home to his embrace. The joy is felt even when the Holy Spirit burns and sears the believer in the purifying crucible of divine love.

There are periods of wonder and awe after such episodes of purgation. My own second period of experimental solitude on the coast opposite the Island of Bardsey in 1983–4 was filled with a spiritual alternation of beautiful sunrises/sunsets and turbulent storms. I have learned complicated evasions and sheer funk in the presence of the fiery God of love, giving rise to existential pain and fear. But the Lord knows every trick and compromise, and was there before me in every turn of the road.

Francis knew well, as I learned, that solitude affords no escape, no diversions, no one to run to, no entertainments or scintillating company or theological argumentation to help me evade the divine demand. But when I surrendered to the God who had lured me into the desert, responding to him in the sanctifying work of purging love, then I found myself lying on the ground in tears of joy. It is in times like these that I have found myself close to Francis in the abandoned and intoxicated way in which he responded to God.

Social and Political Purgation. You do not have to go off into desert solitude to experience this. God deals with us as we are, and where we are. It is also corporate as well as personal, social as well as individual. But there is a web of advertising and sophisticated technological illusion spun around us in the contemporary market-place. We are the victims of market forces in a spiritual sense too. We are often too carnal, lazy, comfortable, and downright sinful to consider the Western rape of the greater part of our poor world.

We shelter under military and nuclear weapons of massive destruction, and are prepared for our governments to finance horrific destruction with arms deals and military expense, provoking further conflict abroad, simply to finance our luxury and save our skins.

It has been part of my hope that the Franciscan life and witness could provide a way forward for our society; an alternative way of living simply, compassionately, and joyously, not promoting guilt but sharing love and reducing our standard of living in order to discover anew life's basic simplicities.

I realize that I am privileged to be part of a community where, as I explore more deeply the way of prayer and solitude, my brothers and sisters are thinking, living, writing, working, protesting, and organizing to alleviate human suffering and contributing to movements for peace and justice. I am but a member of this body, and we are all involved in paying the price of purgation to bring the revolutionary gospel of love and reconciliation to the political and social market-place.

The Franciscan revolution in the thirteenth century shattered the complacency and hypocrisy of the medieval Church, and Pope Innocent III almost bit off more than he could chew when he recognized in Francis the friar he had seen in his dream, his shoulder supporting the tottering Church of the Lateran, for Francis was not in the game of promoting ecclesiastical hierarchical power in a corrupt Christendom.

Apart from our awareness of technological illusion and political justice and peace-making, the work of purgation must involve us in removing the corrupting influences that drug our lives into an addiction which begins with the literal work to be done among addicts of alcohol, tobacco, drugs and chemicals, and the corporate commercialization that flourishes in the production of environmentally deadly pollutants and luxury travel. Our frenetic and hyped-up culture needs the mortification of realizing where all this will lead.

We must not major on guilt and retribution, but there is a salutary truth inbuilt into the natural order that is timely in our present society: 'Do not be deceived; God is not mocked, for you reap whatever you sow.'[7] The text goes on to commend sowing in the field of hope and faith — so let us turn to the next stage in the process.

Illumination

It is possible to be so obsessed with sin and guilt that your spiritual life becomes negative, punitive, and degenerates into a puritanical moral code devoid of spontaneity, freedom, and sheer enjoyment. One of the tests of a genuine spirituality is whether a brother or sister is able to forgive and radiate with real compassion. This indicates the presence of the illuminating joy of the Spirit, and we are reminded of Jesus' words to Peter about forgiving seventy times seven when Francis writes in his *Letter to a Minister*:

> I should like you to prove that you love God and me, his servant and yours, in the following way. There should be no friar in the whole world who has fallen into sin, no matter how far he has fallen, who will ever fail to find your forgiveness for the asking, if he will only look into your eyes. And if he does not ask forgiveness, you should ask him if he wants it. And should he

appear before you again a thousand times, you should love him more than you love me, so that you may draw him to God.[8]

The liberating joy of forgiveness is a real sign of movement from *purgation* to *illumination*. Every morning, as I set out to do my manual work, I have to pass the large cross made of one tree trunk just within my enclosure. I think of John Bunyan's Christian as I pass it, and of the way in which he came to the hill surmounted by the cross, burdened with his pack of sins. As he gazed upon the cross, the pack fell loose and tumbled down the hill into an open sepulchre, as a result of which Christian jumped three times with joy and sang:

> Blest Cross, blest sepulchre,
> Blest rather be
> The Man that was there put to shame for me.

The purgative way has been called the way of beginners; the illuminative way that of the proficient; the unitive way that of the perfect. This is too well-packaged, but it does give the sense of process, movement, and continuity. There was certainly growth to maturity in Francis' life. Every moment of penance was accompanied by the radiance of illumination. It was because of the joy in his heart that Francis walked the path of asceticism, much as an athlete will forgo indulgence in food and drink, practising a disciplined *ascesis* for the sake of the race and the prize.

There are hundreds of flashes and prolonged periods of illumination in the Franciscan saga, and they all led to the initiation into union and identification with Christ that took place on La Verna and accompanied Francis, via Sister Death, into the eternal joy and union with the dazzling glory of God.

The stage of illumination is as far as most of us will get in this life — with flashes of union. Death may intervene, but the process goes on. Sanctification does not end at death, for although our Lord has redeemed us and we are free from sin the other side of death, yet we are not in the state to gaze upon the unveiled glory of the Godhead. There is a beautiful reference to St Francis in Newman's *The Dream of Gerontius*. Gerontius asks his guardian angel: 'Shall I *see* my dearest Master, when I reach his throne?' The angel replies that he does not know what he asks. He *shall* see — for a moment — but that sight will both gladden and pierce the very depths of his soul. Gerontius suddenly feels an overwhelming awe and wonder overtake him. Then the angel says an incredibly beautiful and amazing thing. One mortal, he says, did gaze upon the unutterable glory of the crucified One, and received in his own body the marks of the stigmata — St Francis of Assisi:

> There was a mortal, who is now above
> In the mid glory: he, when near to die
> Was given communion with the Crucified —
> Such, that the Master's very wounds were stamped
> Upon his flesh; and, from the agony
> Which thrilled through body and soul in that embrace,
> Learn that the flame of the Everlasting Love
> Doth burn ere it transform.

In Gerontius' case, the other side of death, there is a deeper *purgation* (now no longer *from* sin, but *to* sanctification), a profounder *illumination*, leading to divine *union* with God in love, which will transform the very structures of his being.

In the earthly experience of Francis, there are moments and episodes of illumination that contain flashes of union — and that is the basis of his undying joy through untold suffering. It is the secret of his simplicity and holiness, the foundation of his perfect joy in tribulation. It is the reason why he can compose the glorious *Canticle of Brother Sun* in blindness and pain.

The three elements, namely, the deepening of repentance, the growth of faith with widening of vision, and experiential union with God, are all present in the simplest and most basic Christian experience. But there is a recurring return to these elements at higher levels, and an intermingling of the stages as the believer grows in grace and loving knowledge of God in Christ.

The San Damiano crucifix experience, at the beginning of Francis' conversion, and the La Verna stigmata, at the end, both reveal this process. There is a humbling awareness of creatureliness and unworthiness, a sense of enlightened adoration, and an identification of union at both places. Look into your own experience and see if you cannot identify some reflection of this process in your own life.

Learn from what seems to be your spiritual infancy that there are moments of growing proficiency, and, by the grace of God, a movement towards maturity and unitive love that will enhance your individuality. The nature of such transformation will unite you in transpersonal communion with God that is ineffable —

which means that before it you are struck dumb with wonder.

If *purgation* sounds somewhat negative, and answers to repentance and stripping of hindrances, then *illumination* answers to faith and vision. Its spectrum is wide, from the first stirring of joy in forgiveness right through to the meditative depths of sharing with Jesus in the gospel life and the contemplative adoration of Christ in the glory of the Father.

It is also a sacramental pilgrimage, based on Scripture, baptism, and Eucharist in the fellowship of the Church. It is dynamic, not static, because there is no affirmation of a body of doctrine without a felt application of heart and mind. The believer *knows* and *feels* the truth, participates in the joys and sorrows of the Jesus way, and allows gospel light to saturate his or her life and overflow in loving relationships. At this stage of illumination, the disciplines of moderate ascetic practice are part of the rule of life, and involvement in social concerns is a consequence.

It is a full and glad life of dedication, with Christ at the centre, overflowing in a sharing of joy and compassion by involvement with others in fellowship and in the alleviation of human suffering and injustices.

All those great 'moments' at the beginning of the friars' journey are moments of illumination. The surrender of Bernard of Quintivalle and the consequent distribution of his wealth; the threefold call as Francis, Bernard, and Peter Catanii opened the missal; the happy journey of the first twelve to see Pope Innocent III; and the amazing, intoxicating joy of life and prayer together in the cattle shed at Rivo Torto before they tumbled out and made their way to the Portiuncula. Turn to your favourite story among the scintillating sources, and see there radiant flashes of illumination as the Holy Spirit shines through the transparent experiences of the first friars and sisters filled with the love of God.

As time goes on, if no barriers are erected, there is growth in yearning love, the glimpses of unitive vision get more intense and the pain of purgation sharper, but all within the illuminative life.[9]

One of my favourite stories that stirs up in me an overflow of love and joy is one in which the *Fioretti* makes it very clear that Francis is *illumined* by the Holy Spirit and treading literally in the footsteps of Christ. Reading this story even today in my hermitage as I write these words, brings me to joy and tears for its simplicity and wonder.

The friars were at the end of their tether trying to minister to a leper, for he was so irritable, impatient, and violent, cursing them and Christ, that they believed he was possessed by an evil spirit.

So the friars came to Francis with great sadness and said they could do no more. Francis, inspired by the Spirit, went to the poor leper and greeted him: 'God give you peace, my dear brother.'

'What peace can I have from God,' retorted the leper, 'who has taken from me all peace and everything that is good, and has made me all rotten and stinking?'

He then opened his heart to Francis, so that the sores of his spirit as well as his body were exposed, and Francis looked, and listened, and loved. The story goes on:

> The leprosy patient said: 'I want you to wash me all over, because I smell so bad that I cannot stand it myself.'
>
> Then St Francis immediately had water boiled with many sweet-scented herbs. Next, he undressed the man with leprosy and began to wash him with his holy hands, while another friar poured the water over him.
>
> And by a divine miracle, wherever St Francis touched him with his holy hands, the leprosy disappeared, and the flesh remained completely healed.
>
> And as externally the water washed his body and the flesh began to heal and be wholly cleansed from leprosy, so too interiorly his soul began to be healed and cleansed. And when the man with leprosy saw himself being healed externally, he immediately began to have great compunction and remorse for his sins. And he began to cry very bitterly. Just as his body was washed with water and cleansed from leprosy, so his conscience was baptised by tears and contrition and cleansed from all evil and sin.
>
> When he was completely washed and healed physically, he was perfectly anointed and healed spiritually. And he was overcome with such compunction and weeping that he humbly accused himself and cried out in a loud voice: 'Woe to me, for I deserve hell for the insults and injuries I have given to the friars and for my impatience and blasphemies against God!'[10]

I'm not sure whether that story moves me so deeply because I am the leper, or whether, like Francis, I long for the beauty and power of Jesus to be incarnate in my life, illuminating my soul and bringing me to the borderland of union with God in love.

Union

Francis always saw grace as the initiating factor in anyone turning to God. Friars who came to him must have a *vocation*, an interior call and movement by the Holy Spirit. Otherwise he would turn them away. No one can live the life of a Christian, a friar, or a sister without the grace of God. So in this mystical journey of *purgation*, *illumination*, and *union*, it begins and ends in God. There is a certain passivity about the embrace of God. Love is infused into the passive soul, for the soul cannot itself generate love, but only respond to it.

The soul gives consent, and that was the attitude which Francis sought in drawing aside into solitude for prayer. The warmth, strength, temper, and enkindling of love belong to God, who draws the soul into union with himself. The consequence is that as God wounds the soul with love, the soul's longings become more unified in God and more withdrawn from the world-system with its illusory quest for money, status, ambition, and power.

The believer does not become vaguely other-worldly in a negative sense, but *more* sensitive to truth, justice, and integrity, and more practically compassionate in a godless world. Genuine mystics like St Theresa and St John of the Cross, the great Carmelites, were indefatigable workers and organizers, yet they not only reach the borderland between illuminative vision and the unitive life, but actually enter the promised land.

There is a sense in which every baptized Christian participates in the life of God and shares that 'mystic sweet communion' with Christ in the fellowship of the Church, which is his body.

As we all share in the trials of *purgation* and the flashes of *illumination*, so *union* in the life of God is communicated to us by his Holy Spirit when we lift our hearts in prayer, when we see God's glory in nature, when we are inspired by Scripture, when we share in the fellowship of fellow human beings, and when we receive the body and blood of Christ in the Eucharist.

But the unitive life of which we are now speaking is that life of sanctity and identification in which the believer enters into a profound union with God, in which the disintegration of our fragmented humanity is healed, in which the soul lives in God, and God in the soul. This is a genuine mutual indwelling, and the *imago Dei*, the *image of God*, is at last healed and restored.

It may mean, as in the case of St Francis, that the believer now lives on two levels of paradox — the outward life seeming to exhibit weakness and physical mortality, while the inward life is more and more possessed by the mystery and fire of God's love. It is not an immediate or instantaneous perfection, but a gradual growth into the maturity of the perfect life. The Orthodox Church calls this experience *epektesis*, and the following quotation is an exposition of Gregory of Nyssa's teaching:

> The idea of epektesis is that the perfect spiritual man is not one who has 'arrived' at a high degree of moral perfection and contemplative knowledge of God. Rather, he is a man who, having attained a high measure, presses on in pursuit of still purer, more vital experience of God's light and truth. The perfect man is the man who is ever moving forward, deeper into the mystery of God. Heaven itself, in this view, consists in an eternal progress into the love and light and life of God, where each fulfilment contains in itself the impulse to further exploration.[11]

The word *ineffable* may be used concerning this third stage of the mystical life. It means that union with God in love is beyond description, beyond words, beyond imagination. The spectrum of such union is so wide that it may be tasted even in this life, but it moves into levels, depths, and dimensions that 'eye has not seen, ear has not heard, neither has it entered into the human heart' to comprehend.

It is difficult to know whether this man or that women, this saint or that mystic, has truly crossed over that border into the realm of mystic communion in God.

But in St Francis of Assisi we have a man in whom finitude and mortality mark him as truly human, and in whom sanctity and holiness mark him as one in whom the Christ-life is transparently present and effective. There is no doubt among his biographers that the seal of God's Spirit upon Francis was physically manifested in the stigmata of La Verna. And to that mystery, as the token of identification with Christ and union with God, we must now turn.

Lord Jesus Christ:
Who when the world was growing cold, to the inflaming of
*   our hearts by the fire of your love, raised up blessèd*
*   Francis, bearing in his body the marks of your passion:*

Mercifully grant to us, your people, true penitence, and
grace to bear the Cross for love of you;
for you live and reign ·with the Father and the Holy Spirit,
one God, now and for ever. Amen.[12]

17 *Stigmata: Union in Love*

FACE TOWARDS LA VERNA

Francis' life was so conformed to the pattern of Jesus that it is clear that he felt the same kind of inevitability toward La Verna as Jesus did in setting his face towards Jerusalem. 'His spirit was drawn towards a rarer atmosphere,' says Cuthbert as he speaks of the mystery and silence that was upon him.

This was the beginning of the last chapter of Francis' life, though the chapter was to last for two years. During that time, he would be more passive in apostolic work because of his mortal weakness, but his influence radiating from his inward life would be more significant. It was a case of God's strength being perfected in Francis' weakness.

As we see this episode unfold, we should be drawn into its interior meaning for our lives, for there is a kind of inevitability in the mingling of suffering and love on this part of the spiritual journey, and God only entrusts such precious experiences to those who have consented to allow the dying and rising of Jesus to become operative in their lives.

Neither Jesus nor Francis were oppressed by this sense of inevitability, for it spoke not of coercion, but of a divine scheme of meaning into which they were drawn for a closer union with God and for the salvation of others. These cannot be separated, for this is no Platonic mystical flight of 'the alone to the Alone', but a mystical participation in redeeming suffering and divine love.

The next paradox on this path is the twofold desire for companions on the one hand and for solitude on the other. Jesus needed the three disciples as he entered into the loneliness of Gethsemane, and Francis needed the seven friars as he contemplated the isolation of La Verna. But neither the three nor the seven could enter into the exposure of such pain and glory — solitude was necessary and primary — but Jesus and Francis needed their disciples simply 'to be there'.

Francis had made this long and exhausting pilgrimage to the mountain, but pilgrimage was not enough. He needed a foundation, a basis upon which to rest as he entered this solitude. So, as before, he turned to the rock of Scripture. At each step in his pilgrimage he had done this, opening Scripture seemingly at random, but three times for confirmation.

After fervent prayer, Francis asked Leo to open the gospel book, and three times it opened at the passion of Christ. So Francis understood that as he had followed Christ in his life, so now he was to enter into the mystery of his suffering.

It was not enough for Francis that he heard and saw in intuition and vision what God was communicating, but he needed to confirm that it was compatible with the written word of Scripture within the fellowship of the Church. Although his experience was intimately personal, it was not subjective, no mere individualistic whim or eccentricity, but grounded rather in the objective revelation of God in Christ. Many of our own mystical flights, if we checked them by such objective revelation, might be seen to be born of imagination or fancy.

GETHSEMANE PRAYER

The next thing we find in this holy and solitary place is that Francis turned to prayer, and the nature of his prayer is pervaded with the same spirit that breathed through Jesus' prayer in Gethsemane. It was the Feast of the Holy Cross, 1224, just before the rising of the sun. Francis knelt before his hut, supported by a rock, and turning east he prayed with tears:

> My Lord Jesus Christ, I pray You to grant me two graces before I die; the first is that during my life I may feel in my soul and in my body, as much as possible, that pain which You, dear Jesus, sustained in the hour of Your most bitter Passion. The second is that I may feel in my heart, as much as possible, that excessive love with which You, O Son of God, were inflamed in willingly enduring such suffering for us sinners.[1]

I have called this his Gethsemane prayer because of its selfless nature. 'Not my will,' prayed Jesus, 'but yours be done.' It was the prayer of abandonment to the will of God, the willingness to be clay in the hands of the potter, to be yielded and submissive to the way of God, wherever it would lead. Francis' prayer was born of the same Spirit, so closely was his will given to Christ.

The first petition asked that he might know physically and spiritually an identification with Jesus' suffering — to be crucified with Christ, so that Christ's passionate love might be manifested in him. This was of a piece with the second petition. It was that he might be inflamed with the same love that caused Jesus to suffer on Calvary for sinners.

This intensely personal prayer of Francis was so close to the gospel, and so biblical in its desire, that we hear echoes of the apostolic words:

> I have been crucified with Christ; and it is no longer I who live, but it is Christ who lives in me.

I want to know Christ and the power of his resurrection and the sharing of his sufferings by becoming like him in his death ...

I am now rejoicing in my sufferings for your sake, and in my flesh I am completing what is lacking in Christ's afflictions for the sake of his body, that is, the church.[2]

This runs counter to the cult of personality fulfilment of some of the more esoteric and New Age spiritualities that have appeared in Christian guise over the last few decades. Profound personal fulfilment *is* to be found in Jesus' way of sacrifice for love's sake, but the element of surrender of egotistic ambitions for the good of another, and of the inevitability of suffering wherever genuine love is found, is integral to the gospel, as it is to the realities of human life.

When a man or woman opens his or her heart to God in so dramatic and naked a manner, then they are taken at their word. Francis was willing to pay the price of suffering love, and this is a mark of the believer who has been united with the will and yearning of God. He knew that whatever suffering was involved, there was sheer joy at the end of the road, for it would mean the salvation of his brothers and sisters, and a sharing of the divine compassion that would ultimately reconcile the whole cosmos to God.

This pulls us up short, for we realize in the light of this apostolic prayer that first of all we do not know what we are saying when we take to ourselves the prayers of the great saints, and second, if we had the slightest idea of what was meant, we would run away from such exposure and surrender of body, mind, and spirit.

THE WOUNDS OF JESUS

For a long time, Francis was held within the tenderness and pity of this prayer. Then, writes Bonaventure:

Suddenly, from the height of heaven, a Seraph having six wings of flame swept down towards him. It appeared in the image of a man hanging on a cross. Two wings at the head, two others served for flight, and the last two covered the body. It was Christ Himself, who, in order to manifest Himself to the blessed one, appeared in this guise. It ... fixed Francis with its gaze, then left him, having imprinted on his flesh the living Stigmata of the Crucifixion. From this moment, indeed, Francis was marked with the wounds of the Divine Redeemer. His feet, his hands seemed pierced with nails of which the round black heads

181

appeared in the palms of the hands, and on the feet, the points thrust through the flesh bent back. And there, too, on the right side, was a wound as though made by a lance, from which the blood frequently oozed, even through his shirt and tunic.[3]

The primitive sources are at one concerning the fact of the stigmata, albeit with divergences of detail, but there is a fascinating interplay between 'what happened' and 'what it meant'.

In spite of the visible wounds, Francis at first tried to hide them. But then he turned to his companions and asked them in veiled terms whether one should reveal or hide an extraordinary favour that God had granted.

Illuminato saw that Francis was filled with strange joy and perplexity, and said: 'Brother, remember that when God reveals his secrets to you, it is not for yourself alone; they are intended for others too.'[4]

Bonaventure goes on to say that Francis was aware that there were certain things he had learned in that mysterious encounter that could never be shared with anyone on earth, but then he timidly shared with his companions what had happened, yet avoided showing the wounds, which he tried to hide in bandages and in the sleeves of his habit.[5]

Leo and Rufino at times changed his habit and bathed his wounds from necessity, and others caught sight of the evidence of them. Then, as Bonaventure said: 'More than fifty friars with St Clare and her nuns and innumerable lay people saw them after his death. Many of them kissed the stigmata and felt them with their own hands, to prove the truth.'[6]

Francis realized how painfully and tenderly God had dealt with him, and was filled with immense gratitude, for even the very ground of La Verna became sacred and precious to him. The smiting by the Seraph filled him with wonder and put him in mind of the Angel of the Lord smiting Jacob in the dislocating of his thigh during the wrestling night of prayer, bringing him to a surrender of love. Then Francis got Leo or Rufino to consecrate the stone upon which the Seraph had stood, as Jacob had consecrated the stone of his vision at Bethel, washing and anointing it with oil.[7]

THE MEANING OF THE STIGMATA

At the conclusion of his fiery and passionate letter to the Galatians, the apostle Paul enters into a profound sense of, and desire for, peace.

He glories in the cross of Christ by which he has been crucified to the world and the world to him. He prays peace and mercy upon all who follow in this way, and before blessing his readers with the grace of Christ, he asks that no one should trouble him any longer, because he bears the *stigmata* of Jesus in his body.[8] I think that St Paul was meaning the scars of beatings and persecution he had undergone in the loving service of the Saviour, but the same word *stigmata* is used for his scars as for Francis' Calvary wounds.

The meaning of both is the same. They serve as a seal of God's merciful and loving approval in suffering and identification with Jesus. They are intimately connected with the redeeming work of Christ on the cross for the redemption of the world, and they cannot be separated from his resurrection in glory.

There is a sense in which the apostle Paul and the Poverello Francis are very special saints, but this is the place to remind ourselves that *all* God's people are saints by virtue of his grace, and all are called into the way of the dying and rising of Jesus.

The meaning of the stigmata for Francis is to ·be seen in the context of his quest for personal identity and his desire to be wholly identified in loving union with Christ. He likened the experience to the two powerful confrontations of Jacob with God in the book of Genesis. The first was at Bethel, where he dedicated and anointed the stone from which 'Jacob's ladder' began to ascend, and at Peniel, where the mysterious Angel of the Lord wrestled in solitude and darkness with the patriarch through the night. The Seraph that appeared comes straight out of Isaiah 6.2, though it was at the same time the crucified Saviour.

Jacob was searching for his own identity as a Bethel-pilgrim when God opened up the traffic between heaven and earth, and later at Peniel he yearned to know the name of the divine wrestler.

When Leo secretly spied on Francis before the Feast of the Holy Cross, he found him in the woods, kneeling in the moonlight, with face and arms uplifted to heaven, repeating with fervour: 'Who are you, my dearest God? And who am I, a vile worm and your useless servant?' Then, as Leo looked on in awe and fear, he saw a flame of fire descend and envelop Francis.

This brings together the night of wrestling Jacob and the quest for identity expressed in that marvellous hymn of Charles Wesley, containing the stanzas:

Come, O thou Traveller unknown
  Whom still I hold, but cannot see;
My company before is gone,
  And I am left alone with thee;
With thee all night I mean to stay
And wrestle till the break of day.

I need not tell thee who I am,
  My misery and sin declare;
Thyself hast called me by my name,
  Look on thy hands and read it there:
But who, I ask thee, who art thou?
Tell me thy name, and tell me now.[9]

The stigmata experience of Francis was not a selfish pursuit of a coveted identity, but a confirmation of the truth and the seal of God, for from his conversion Francis had always sought and found his identity in God. It is only as we discover who we are within the love of God that we are able to experience our own integration and become reconcilers and peacemakers among those around us.

Even at the beginning of his pilgrimage, Francis spent the whole night in Bernard of Quintivalle's house, repeating those sacred words as a holy mantra: *Deus meus et Omnia* — 'My God and my All.' Bernard, who had been feigning sleep, realized that Francis was wholly taken up, and possessed by, God. He also felt himself drawn by the power of the Holy Spirit radiating through the holy man. The *Fioretti* tells the story, overflowing with the fervour and emotion that possessed both Francis and Bernard at the beginning of the great adventure.[10]

IDENTIFICATION WITH CHRIST AND THE WORLD

The fascination and mystery of Francis' stigmata has captured the imagination of theologians, mystics, and poets from the thirteenth century onwards. A collection of the best poetry, and prose, pruned of sentimentality, would yield many layers of meaning.

One poem that would have to be included is by the Anglican priest-missionary Arthur Shearley Cripps, who was dearly loved by his adopted African people. His poetry not only enters into the primal vision of African religion, but also into a profound mystical and human interpretation of the stigmata of St Francis.

The poem is called *The Death of St Francis*, and in it Francis himself expresses the impossibility of communicating the sacred wonder of the wounding on Mount La Verna. 'How can I tell it?' he asks:

> The thing is sacred, dear, –
> Hands grew to hands, feet seemed to grow to feet,
> His Hands to my hands, Feet of His to mine;
> Exalted and extended on His cross,
> I seemed in one great stab of eager pain
> To feel His heart beating within my heart ...
>
> I cannot tell the half of it, yet hear
> What rush of feeling still comes back to me,
> From that proud torture hanging on His Cross,
> From that gold rapture of His Heart in mine.

Then there is an amazing shift in Francis' identification *with* Christ in his passion, to an identification *in* Christ, taking to himself the suffering and darkness of the world's sin:

> I knew in blissful anguish what it means
> To be a part of Christ, and feel as mine
> The dark distresses of my brother limbs,
> To feel it bodily and simply true,
> To feel as mine the starving of His poor,
> To feel as mine the shadow of curse on all,
> Hard words, hard looks, and savage misery,
> And struggling deaths, unpitied and unwept.
> To feel rich brothers' sad satieties,
> The weary manner of their lives and deaths,
> That want in love, and lacking love lack all.
> To feel the heavy sorrow of the world
> Thicken and thicken on to future hell,
> To mighty cities with their miles of streets,
> Where men seek work for days, and walk and starve,
> Freezing on river-banks on winter nights,
> And come at last to cord or stream or steel.

The poem moves through the darkness, malice, and black hideousness of human sin and cruelty – feeling, bearing, atoning for it all, then bursts forth in forgiveness and divine love.

Francis, in Christ, sees, pities, understands, and bears all the sadness, waste, and emptiness of human sin and sorrow, and pours out heart-felt mercy in drawing sinners home to reconciling love:

> O Heart of Jesus, Sacred, Passionate,
> Anguish it was, yet anguish that was bliss,
> To love them heart to heart, each selfish heart,
> To clasp them close, and pray in utter truth —
> 'Father, forgive, they know not what they do.'
> One was the heart of him that ground the poor,
> Poor weary heart, so blinded and misled!
> One was the heart of her that reeked in shame,
> Poor weary heart, so blinded and misled!
> One was my heart, that wasted half its years,
> And knew so little how to use the rest
> To God's sole glory, and the love of men,
> Poor weary heart, so blinded and misled!

And then, wonder of wonders, Francis in Christ confronts the malignant source of satanic hatred that pollutes and corrupts human weakness. With one awful thrill of fire and ecstasy, he destroys the hatred of Satan and is pierced in hands, feet, and side with the wounds of Calvary:

> And O! that Sacred Heart burnt up in Flame
> Against that harsh misleader of our world,
> And O! I felt an awful thrill of Love
> As with one heart-beat of wild ecstasy
> I set my heel upon that Serpent's head
> In resolute anguish, watching how the fangs
> Snapped at my heel, and gored it into blood,
> My heel that yet shall grind his head to dust.
> Was it I that did it? Nay, the Christ in me,
> But when I woke His Prints were in my hands,
> And in my feet, while in my side there showed
> As it were the Heart-Wound from the soldier's lance.[11]

CHRIST INCARNATE IN FRANCIS

Francis entered into union with Christ in love. In such a life, he suffered in and with Christ, took to himself the pains and sorrows of his brothers and sisters, and then confronted the powers of darkness at their source. This is what the gospel meant to Francis, and that is what it must mean for us.

Christ becomes incarnate in the believer, and the way in which our response to God's call is lived out becomes our personal vocation. For some, it will be an apostolic life of preaching and prayer; for others, a mystical life of contemplation. For some, it will be a missionary call to the ends of the earth — perhaps with the suffering of martyrdom to crown it; for others, it will be a faithful living out of home, family, and involvement with agencies of compassion, peace, and justice. Life stories may vary greatly, but all God's people are called to incarnate Christ in the world.

These last two chapters have been concerned with the mystical path of *purgation, illumination,* and *union.* As this process was lived out in Francis' life, it became clear that it was rooted in love for God and love for creation. This means that far from the mystical path revealing a Platonic, ethereal and other-worldly aloofness from common humanity, it was compassionate and practical. In Francis' day it meant, among other things, caring for lepers, and in our day it should mean caring for all the victims of our contemporary world.

When Enzo Natta, the Italian journalist, interviewed Franco Zeffirelli, maker of the film *Brother Sun, Sister Moon,* Zeffirelli criticized hippie pseudo-mystics and affirmed the ascetic and social dimensions of the Franciscan vision. He maintained that Francis sought inner perfection through renunciation, sacrifice, and service for others, and went on:

Hippies have the opposite attitude. They want to find perfection in a lazy way of life, to pluck apples from trees they have not tended, to drink pure water from unguarded streams, to fornicate and go their careless way. And they call that Franciscanism? The worst of it is that many of them think it is really so, and for that reason I have tried to play a trick on these false mystics in my *Brother Sun, Sister Moon.* Up to a certain point in the film I let them believe that they are right, that they are like St Francis. Later they are shown the difference, the profound difference, that separates them from the Poor Man of Assisi. The difference arises from the obstinate fact that in real life nothing comes as a gift without strings, and that sacrifice is the coin in which we must pay for things worth having.[12]

Let the last word in this chapter come from Francis Thompson, who touches upon the heart of the matter in his poem 'Franciscus Christificatus:'

Thou who thoughtest thee too low
For His priest, thou shalt not so
'Scape Him and unpriested go!
In thy hand thou wouldst not hold Him,
In thy flesh thou shalt enfold Him;
Bread wouldst not change into Him ... ah see!
How He doth change Himself to thee![13]

Lord Jesus Christ:
The wounds of your passion are now the wounds of your
glory;
And your servant Francis bore those wounds with tears and
with love;
Grant that in our earthly pilgrimage we may be allowed some
small share in your passion,
That at the last we may enter into your joy;
For your dear name's sake. Amen.

18 ❧ *Francis and Franciscans*

FRANCIS THE CHRIST-BEARER

In writing this book, I've been in touch with Franciscans of all three Orders, and with some of our Companions of the Society of St Francis.

The thing that impresses me most is that they are such an assortment of individuals, with a wide spectrum of diversity of temperament, and yet with a wholehearted enthusiasm and response to St Francis.

Among them are fervent activists for justice and peace, enthusiastic evangelists seeking to share Christ in a secular society, profoundly contemplative people seeking a way to live the life of prayer alone or in small groups, and others fired with an openness towards other faiths in an increasingly pluralist world.

The person of Francis is the catalyst for prayer and action, and the most precious thing about him is that he incarnated Christ in a remarkable manner, so that there is no teaching or spirituality apart from his person. It would be impossible to take away Francis and be left with a *corpus* of teaching that could stand on its own. In this sense, too, Francis is like Christ. Christianity *is* Christ, and wherever 'Christian teaching' is separated from the Saviour it becomes mere religion, and either is boring and irrelevant or may be used for political and power-structure ends which betray both Christ and Francis.

One of our tertiaries speaks of Francis' impact on his own life:

> St Francis often appears to be quite naive and, in that, he is totally disarming. He did not get involved in theological dispute or argument, but in his own simplicity he spoke and lived the Gospel directly. Often he is a frightening example of the full implications of living by the Gospel, and yet he softens it all and makes it most appealing through his love for all created things. His care and concern for people, his embrace of the leper, his fearlessness with Gubbio's wolf, his crazily bold 'I am the herald of the great king' to the brigands who robbed him, his Canticle of the Sun; in all this terrible directness and tender love Francis is a whole, complex, many-faceted personality who is a complete imitator of the Christ he loves, and at the same time a recognisable modern man with whom I can identify. He says to me, 'Come on, you can do it like this!'

During the writing of this book, I have been living in my hermitage in the grounds of Tymawr Convent, and one of the sisters has just returned from Assisi. In her meditation on *Pilgrimage*, she speaks of holy places as graced by the presence of Christ, and of the life-changing experience that such a pilgrimage can make. It is like climbing a mountain and then gazing down at the wonderful scenery below. There is the strenuous effort to get to the top, the pure joy of the achievement, and the delicious feeling of awe in surveying God's creation. The aching limbs, laboured breath, and fear of falling are all forgotten as they are gathered into the joy:

> So it was for me at Assisi where, after a long journey, I knelt before the crucifix of St Damian which had spoken to St Francis: 'Go, Francis, and repair my house because it is falling into ruin', and later when I visited the little chapel, the Portiuncula, where Francis began his great work for God, where he was joined by the first friars of his Order and where St Clare came to make her vows to God. The deep warm silence in both places was full of joyous wonder and thanksgiving for all that St Francis and St Clare had been and done and for the legacy they had left for us to inherit.

She goes on to say that you cannot stay on the mountaintop or sit still at a crucifix. The world below calls out in its need, as when Jesus descended from the Mount of Transfiguration. But the vision of Christ is carried down the mountain, and the inspiration of Francis is one that becomes our own interior vision.

DIFFERENT FACETS OF FRANCIS

A. felt drawn, by Francis' example, to be a doctor, but this was after looking at him for some years, and the growing appreciation of Francis is evident in what he says:

> As a child I was attracted to the stories of Francis and the animals and birds — I saw him as a gentle person at home with nature. I too was like this and deeply wished to be more alone with God's creatures.
>
> At the age of thirteen a friar preached in our church about Francis and the lepers and a whole new facet was added — of course people are also God's creatures! I knew then that I too must work with lepers, to care for people, to be a doctor. This to me, at thirteen years, was God's will.

191

Later I understood Francis' desire to follow the Master as closely as possible in the way the early disciples were sent out. I understood his total poverty — his desire to have nothing between himself and God's will — his desire for his life to be owned and ruled by God.

The challenge of poverty is one that we all feel. It has split the Franciscan Order from earliest times, because Francis was more strict than Jesus in his attitude towards money. He held to personal and communal poverty, and the tensions within the First Order caused much schism and heartache as some friars held to a literal following of Francis and others used their talents in teaching, medical missions, and scholarly pursuits. The Second Order of Poor Clares always sought to live according to the primitive practice of poverty, and of course the Third Order, involving family life, education of children, and work and witness within the wider world, has kept the principle of poverty as a guide.

I have been among those who have bewailed the influence of television in some of our friaries, the multiplication of computers, and jetting around the world for conferences. It is easier to criticize than to be constructive, and what does one say to a group of dedicated tertiaries who have mortgages to pay, run two cars for husband and wife in professional work, and whose children demand video games that encourage machismo (or intergalactic) violence? One of our Third Order members explodes in the face of the materialism of Christians:

> Possessions are our own lack of faith — 'God will let me die if I don't stock food, have clothes, a job, money in the bank.' Francis trusted that God would care for him — not give him a long life, comfort, life assurance. Without possessions which are burdens, we are free to live fully exposed to all life's extremes of joy and sorrow, and above all, freed to do God's will rather than our own.

FRANCISCANS ARE A DANGEROUS THREAT

Dissatisfaction with the nominal Church (and nominal Franciscanism) is found among the followers of St Francis. It has always been thus. Take this, from one Franciscan who echoes others in the same vein:

St Francis would probably be appalled by SSF which has basi-
cally become too institutionalised. The only portion of SSF
retaining any hope is the *Companions*, a hopelessly disorganised
group who merely wish to live in the spirit of the Gospel in the
way St Francis did.

I am constantly told that there is more concern for bureaucracy
and revision of the constitution than for the poor and outcasts of
our society. One group bewailed that there was more spirituality
among their Buddhist friends than in the Franciscan group, which
tempted them to leave.

It became humorous with yet another group, one of whom told
me that he was thinking of leaving the Third Order, for, 'Why
follow the servant when you can follow the Master?' But then he
went on:

At the last local meeting (there were four of us), I expressed the
sentiment that I would leave, and it transpired that the other three
were thinking of resigning too, to escape the encumbrance of the
rules and hierarchy and to really try to follow Christ. This left
no one to receive our resignation, so seeing we all want to follow
Christ, we have stayed together. It is only when you don't want
to be a Franciscan that you can become one.

As I listen to these criticisms, some of which I share, I find that
they are not carping, negative, and destructive, but are the result of
simply doing what Christ and Francis told us to do – bring gospel
values to bear upon our own beliefs and practices. So it is heart-
warming to find humour mixed with criticism, and then to see that
those sometimes accused of bureaucracy or of lacking in vision are
the very ones to reveal a hidden Christlikeness that displays true
poverty of spirit, reaching out to the outcasts on the margins of
our society.

There is a school of Franciscan thought that follows the scholar
Paul Sabatier in seeing Cardinal Hugolino as 'the very soul of the
group who are compromising the Franciscan ideal'.[1] Yet in one of
the sermons of Bonaventure we are told that when Hugolino became
Pope Gregory IX, he sought to bring his life into conformity with
the gospel obedience of Francis. In one of his rooms in the papal
palace, he housed a leper, and, wearing the Franciscan habit, served,
fed, and nursed him. One day, being extremely tired, the pope was
slow, and the leper commented: 'Has the pope no one other than

an old man to look after me?' He had not realized that it was the pope who served him each day.[2]

This paradox is further illustrated when Franciscans of the three Orders make their pilgrimage to Assisi and enter the amazing, beautiful, aesthetic, and architecturally breath-taking Basilica and Convent of St Francis in Assisi, knowing that the Poverello and his companions in utter poverty are buried there.

Then they make their journey down to the tiny Portiuncula chapel, which stands, not now in a green forest, but inside the stupendous Basilica of Santa Maria dei Angeli.

The problem reaches right back to the early days. One day after Francis' death, Leo ran to Giles at Perugia, crying: 'There is a marble vase set up at Assisi; and they throw money into it by order of Elias, to build a great rich convent for the brothers who have vowed to be poor like Francis!'

'Let them build a convent as long as from here to Assisi,' replied Giles. 'My little nook is enough for me.' But Leo could not take it lying down, so he rushed up to where the vase had been placed and smashed it with a hammer. Elias acted immediately – Leo was beaten with rods and exiled from Assisi.

Giles looked on with sorrow and scorn as he saw the friars getting fat and sleek, mocking the poverty of Francis. One day, another brother rushed to him, crying: 'Good news! Good news!' 'Tell it, my son,' responded Giles. 'In a vision I was taken to hell and I saw there not a single brother of the Order.'

Giles replied with a sigh and a strange smile. 'Yes,' went on the friar, 'there are none there, or if there are, why did I not see them?'

'Because you didn't go deep enough!' was the brutal answer.[3]

On the one hand we hear of genuine Franciscans speaking with sorrow of the great compromise of the life and simple gospel rule of their father Francis by Brother Elias and Cardinal Hugolino. And on the other we hear other genuine Franciscans speaking with thankfulness of the far-sightedness, courage, and ability of these two who understood the necessity of preserving Francis' spiritual vision and spreading his message through the Church and the world in perpetuating the threefold Franciscan Order through the ages.

The problem is not so much contradiction as paradox, for there are men and women of holiness in both camps, and there are fanatics and schismatics among the 'Spirituals' as there are arrogant and unspiritual scholars and bureaucrats among the 'Conventuals'.

It is interesting that in the next generation from Francis, the friar Jacopone da Todi, whose sympathies were with the *zelanti* Spirituals, actually joined the *mitigati* friars of the relaxed rule in Todi.[4]

One of our sisters recently wrote to me, speaking of the way in which she felt the pattern of the incarnation in our life brought integration of gospel and social values together, revealing the way in which the Franciscan community could bear witness to the fragmented society around us.

She speaks of the way in which the *life* of Francis (and therefore of Christ) shines in our Franciscan witness. This is seen in such values as simple joy in life, inspiring spontaneity, a deepening life of prayer, a love of the whole created order, a concern for reconciliation among warring factions, and practical work among the socially unacceptable of our time. Belonging to the Franciscan family continually brings these values to life, and she is constantly challenged and sustained by the rest of the family of Francis.

One of our tertiaries, who is professionally involved in education and leads a mountaineering expedition for sixth formers every year, makes regular retreats at Glasshampton monastery. He wrote to me to express his continuing engagement with a spirituality spelled out by Francis in his personal, family, and professional life – keeping it all together.

Basic factors for him are the simple living that Francis enjoined in harmony with the environment, love for all living creatures, which must lead us to care for our planet, and avoidance of overproduction and consumption.

For him, Francis' witness to poverty points to some practical level of identification with the poor, the powerless, and the oppressed of the world, but is careful to avoid compassion fatigue, which preserves Franciscan joy. He finds a gentleness and non-violence in Francis that corresponds with the *Satyagraha* of Gandhi, and all this is based upon a life of prayer in which Francis centred himself in the indwelling Christ.

RECIPROCAL FELLOWSHIP

Over the last fifteen years, I have known real fellowship in joy and pain with a friend who has lived for long periods in one of our friaries in appreciation of the Franciscan ethos, and who has emerged from psychiatric illness into healing and living faith in Christ.

I have been of help to him along the way, and especially recently he has reciprocated such help to me. His life story could so easily be set in the context of Franciscan joy and pain, sensitivity to creation, and the profound work of Christ's redemption. His most recent letter sounds genuine Franciscan notes of the mingling fellowship of human weakness and simple trust as we sustain one another in prayer:

Openly to confess and acknowledge one's suffering before God, one's weakness, sadness, badness, inadequacy and grief, is of the essence of being human: to do so before another is an act which, while it requires courage, faith and trust, does permit and make possible an ever-deepening tenderness, sensitivity and compassionate lovingness of relationship which is one of the greatest blessings of the human condition. It seems to me that what God loves best is to sweep into our sorrowful penitence and tembling contrition and irradiate it with His unutterable joy and peace. In human terms you as an agent of God have often had something of that effect upon me; and perhaps all I can offer in return is the assurance that it does work, and that it is real, and that it is at that point that both God and the human being are most truly and deeply themselves in relation to each other.

This sense of personal wounds and suffering is reflected in another of our sister's experience, when she says:

Because the wounds in my past, though healed, are still tender, I try not to look back, unless by doing so God enables me to help someone with similar, though unhealed, wounds. I used to think that one's wounds were healed when this occurs. Now I would go further than this and say that they are only healed when one can say, and honestly mean, 'Thank you, God, for that experience which has brought me into a relationship with you that would not otherwise have been possible.'

Then she goes on to speak of the way in which Francis, under God, led her into deeper fellowship with him and into the Franciscan life:

So I am looking back to my first contact with St Francis. This began when I was old enough to read and enjoy my Mother's books. She died when I was nine. I still have her copy of *The Legend of St Francis* by the Three Companions. When I was newly at university I bought *The Chronicles of Brother Wolf* by Tertius, Friar and Servant and St Francis. In the context of a story this taught me a lot. Together these books probably set my feet towards the Franciscan way. About this time one of the first Anglican friars preached at our church. I was impressed, but I recall my father saying that it was most impractical!

It was many years before I had my next contact with Franciscans. I had a busy and quite difficult life and was also very isolated spiritually. Then I met a friar and a tertiary on a church pilgrimage to the Holy Land and when I learned about the Third Order, I knew this was what I had been searching for. So I suppose that my first attraction was to the companionship of those with a similar spiritual outlook. Then as now I thank God for their joy, their simplicity and above all, for their love for our dear Lord Jesus Christ and in him, their love for all mankind and all of creation.

But the demands of the gospel life go even deeper. We have seen that when Francis was drawn to La Verna, he was faced with confrontation with dark, cosmic powers and drawn into the love and suffering of Jesus' conflict and victory on Calvary. So J.'s letter continues:

I came to be drawn more and more into silence and solitude, but at the same time I am drawn into people's needs and hurts. This sharing of their wounds is drawing me more and more into an awareness of Christ's wounds, into the cosmic conflict that is being waged between Good and Evil, in face of the victory which was won at Calvary.

My life is taking on a rhythm of periods of silence and solitude, spent on the holy island of Bardsey (Ynys Enlli in Welsh) which is situated off the Lleyn Peninsula in North Wales. It has a very long history as a place where Celtic saints lived and died and it remains a place where God seems very powerfully present. Then I return to be engulfed in all sorts of activities for the Third Order and for my family who give me much joy, especially the grandchildren!

COMMUNITIES OF HEALING AND PRAYER

This principle of deeper into Calvary love in prayer and deeper into human compassion in service stirs the Franciscan heart, for it is the expression of love for God and for our fellows.

Some of our Third Order members have spoken with me about the desire to form a small community of First Order brothers and sisters with Third Order families, and an openness to people who are in need of various levels of healing. I have warmed to such an expression of Franciscan life where there would be a life of prayer at the heart of such a community, a daily celebration of the Eucharist, together with all the joy, fellowship, and service of ordinary human life around it. Families and individuals could share as much as they wanted of the spiritual centre, and young single or committed young couples could share this vocation for a year or more.

Quite apart from its witness as an extended family in the midst of the present disintegrating poverty of our society, various priorities could emerge. In one place a particular work of caring for homeless people may develop, and in another a centre of healing where nursing and sacramental divine healing would become part of its ministry. As one Franciscan comments about such a venture:

> It is as though Francis would turn the whole of life upside down. Instead of the attitude of 'what's in it for me?' he would put the claims of Christ, to see each person as a dear member of our own family, to reverence each bit of God's creation and to find joy in it all.

Seven years ago, among the men who lived for extended periods at our Hilfield friary was one who shared some of his joys and perplexities with me, and who wrote retrospectively about that time. It expressed the positive joy that living in an accepting, stable community meant to him, of the warmth of welcome, the release from pressure, and the ability to put down roots into a space that had been freely given him.

The friary offered a pattern of simple and modest living, no competitive harassment, but daily communal routine. There was daily worship, which was free and not obligatory, and an easy yet defined, disciplined routine in which brothers and sisters mixed with guests, long-stay members, and wayfarers.

Even for people with no personal meaning or sense of purpose, the whole atmosphere drew one into its own meaning, which had to do with love, compassion, and humour − and ultimately with God. This fellow would also have found other aspects of community life in our smaller urban houses, equally valid but different, some of them mixed and busy houses. But for him, at that time, Hilfield, and later Glasshampton, were what he needed.

This is the kind of healing and reconciling community that I can envisage, so that the broad mix of friars and sisters and the tertiary singles and families would represent the 'core' of the community with a real place for different kinds of people who could share in the life, work, and worship of a Christ-centred family that did not push religion, but shared in wholeness and joy.

We would sometimes fail in the endeavour, but the ideal is expressed in what that young man wrote about his experience:

> Agreeable surroundings and the absence of everyday stress are not enough. What is special about SSF is that it is a community of people trying to live together in love, and united by a common aim and focus. I sometimes feel that just as it is only other people who can do you real psychic or emotional harm, so it is only other people who can repair the damage. For someone like me, SSF is in the business of repairing the damage. It does so by the consistent practise of a love of which sensitivity, tolerance, respect and emotional discipline are component features. Also there is among the brothers a powerful instinct to seize on the positive aspect of things, however negligible it may seem, and to emphasize what is good while forgiving the bad. This tends to remove most of the harshness, ill temper and stridency one finds in everyday life, with a consequently heartening and mellowing effect on all within the community.

Being a Franciscan, I must not forget animals! Brother Amos took over from me as Guardian when I left Glasshampton to explore the hermit life in 1990. He knew I missed Mungo, our monastery dog, so I was very moved when I received this word from him:

> If you would like Mungo, of course you could have him, but he has quite a ministry here and he might feel he's not putting his talents fully to use in the Lord's work. He loves his hours of prayer on the lawn in the garth, but equally he realises his responsibility to those who need an ear in their hand for a bit, or for their health, need to be cajoled into going for a walk. His patient humility when being cursed by those who dislike him is an example I would not be without.

I didn't take up the offer, but I looked at the brown habited picture of Mungo, a real Franciscan dog, on my hermitage wall, with wistfulness!

FRANCISCANS AND THE HERMIT VOCATION

There is already some praying and thinking taking place concerning the development of a vocation to the hermit life within the Third Order. We are accustomed to Third Order Franciscans engaging actively in the world, surrounded by families, friends, and dependants, and busily engaged in compassionate service. But it was among tertiaries that many hermit vocations arose in the early days, completely consistent with the Franciscan vocation, for the one body has many members, and some of them are hidden and contemplative. Francis himself wrote a rule, *Religious Life in Hermitages*[5] for the use of First and Third Order brothers and sisters.

Francis himself always felt drawn to remote places and caves; and even after the first twelve friars had returned from having the 1209 rule approved by Pope Innocent III, they debated whether they should live as hermits or follow a mixed life of prayer and work for the salvation of souls.[6]

It became clear that the First Order friars should live a mixed life with a profound emphasis on prayer, but with joyful preaching of the good news of Jesus. Nevertheless, many First Order friars, especially among the later Spirituals, lived semi-eremitical or completely solitary lives.

When John of Parma resigned as Minister General in 1257, he retired to the hermitage of Greccio, and his life and that of Angelo of Clareno influenced many members of the Third Order scattered over Italy who were living in solitide or small hermitages.[7]

It may seem very strange to frenetically active Christians that God is calling people to a disciplined life of prayer and solitude in these days when dark powers of violence and injustice are rampant in our world. There are those who are called to a life of direct social and non-violent political action; others to an apostolate of medical and material aid to victims of war, exile, and 'ethnic cleansing'; and others to a life of prayer and reparation on behalf of these people.

It is a great joy to me to discover people in the Third Order who are feeling the stirrings of such a vocation, though they may be unable to understand what is happening. 'As they grow in awareness of God, they may be drawn into the cosmic battle between good and evil,' writes one of our tertiaries. 'They certainly will be drawn into sharing the suffering of others and intercession will become very costly. Involvement in the spiritual warfare in heavenly places can be very frightening.'

That last sentence indicates something of the dangers of wandering into solitude in obedience to what could well be a subjective desire that has arisen from unexamined roots. There must be some kind of examination, support, and encouragement from a mature group who sustain the brother or sister in such an exploration, as well as some practical and theological guidance from those who have themselves participated in such a vocation. In a paper on the eremitical life written by one of our tertiaries, the point is made:

> Hermits in Religion always have the support of their Order and permission for their way of life is only given after a completed noviciate and some time in community. There is a time of testing of the vocation and this principle should be followed by the Third Order. I know that many tertiaries are a pretty independent lot ... but we all live under obedience! It may be that some guidelines can be drawn up. We want them to remain in the family of the Third Order, to be part of the community, so perhaps they should be asked to attend the one area meeting when Renewals take place each year. But before all this, perhaps there should be some sort of commissioning. We must recognise that there may be a rhythm of periods of withdrawal for the purposes of prayer followed by more active service and participation in the world, as our father Francis was led to do.

Cecily Hallack and Peter Anson, when discussing Third Order hermits, raise the question why these men and women chose an Order intended to serve God spiritually and socially in the marketplace of the world. Why didn't they join one of the religious Orders intended for those with an eremitical vocation?

> The answer appears to be a very human one: that these men and women fell in love with the Franciscan spirit, and being drawn more to the solitary life rather than to that of the Friars Minor or the Poor Clare, asked humbly for the habit of the Third Order, with the determination to add privately what they would to the quite considerable austerity of the Rule of the Order of Penance.[8]

THE BREADTH OF FRANCISCAN WITNESS

If 'the world is our cloister', this is certainly reflected in our magazine *The Franciscan.*[9] There, is presented a spread of news of participation in Franciscan faith and witness, with an exciting human dimension that has its hidden roots in prayer.

Pain and suffering are reflected in the brothers and sisters who are involved in ministering to the homeless, people affected with HIV and AIDS, victim support, and such groups and agencies as the L'Arche Community.

Brother Benedict smiles out of an article on the joys and sorrows of the Glasgow house, and Sister Joyce mischievously grins above the item that tells us that the sisters' noviciate operates from the contrasts of noisy and joyful Brixton and the calm beauty of Compton Durville, Somerset.

In the September 1992 issue, there is a glorious picture of a joyful crowd of professed, novices, postulants, and aspirants from the Hautambu Friary in the Solomon Islands, and a terrifying picture of an American armoured tank backed by columns of flames illustrating Sister Helen Julian's article on 'Peace and Justice' in the following issue.

Roman Catholic and Anglican friars working together with Methodists in Leeds is refreshing ecumenical news, and I can imagine the excitement and laughter shared by two of our Anglican SSF brothers when they attended the conference in Assisi entitled 'Young Religious of the Franciscan Families'.

Perhaps we are endeavouring to do too much, and are spread too thinly across the immense areas of human need. But all our brothers and sisters of the three Orders and Companions are one in their dedication to Christ and the life of prayer.

Let me close this chapter with two pertinent quotations. The first is from Brother Anselm's moving words on the day when we finally gave up St Francis' School for Boys at Hooke, which dear Father Owen had founded forty years ago:

Nobody has found a way for taking leave of around 200 people individually, meaningfully — and simultaneously. When it's time to go all you can do is smile at those nearest to you, and slip quietly away — very conscious of the fact that there will be no more Open Days, that you can't think to yourself 'Oh well, there's always next time, I'll say it then' — but with a stronger awareness of the very powerful significance of Hooke for anyone who was a part of it and of the permanence of Hooke for us, and of Hooke as something we can in a sense share with others — even though the swimming pool is empty and the place is up for sale.

The second is a typically Franciscan encouragement in which Sister Cecilia writes in her 'Minister's Letter', grounding SSF's work for peace and justice firmly at the heart of the gospel; and we conclude with the prayer Cecilia uses, bringing Francis and Franciscans together in the inspiration of Christ:

Justice for the Christian proclaims that everyone has value in the sight of God, who confronts and challenges us with the less recognisable injustice engendered by prejudice, Phariseeism, racism, class barriers and exclusivism. We have to look at the violence within ourselves, while deploring the violence which brutalises, tortures and maims.

As Christians, and especially as Franciscans, we must be on guard against thinking in terms of, and the claiming of rights for, ourselves. We have no rights; all is gift. All that comes to us is a trust and belongs to God. There are no rights in the dominion of heaven except the right to receive the unutterable and inexhaustible love of God revealed in Jesus and the right to offer to God through the Holy Spirit all that we are and have. To expect and seek rights makes mockery of the total Christ event, for God in Jesus surrendered all rights; our Lord claimed nothing except 'Abba, Father.'

Keep us faithful, O God, to the inspiration of blessèd Francis,
that seeking nothing for ourselves, we may bring true riches to the world;
Through him who gave us himself, Jesus Christ our Saviour. Amen.

Epilogue: 🌿
Francis — Universal Brother

Towards the end of *The Book of the Lover and the Beloved*, Ramon Lull tells of the Lover wandering into a monastic cloister. The monks ask if he is a *Religious*. 'Yes,' he answers, 'of the Order of my Beloved.'

They enquire what rule he follows. 'The rule of my Beloved,' he replies. Then he is asked to whom he is vowed. 'To my Beloved,' he says. The monks then ask if he follows his own will. 'No,' he says again, 'it is given to my Beloved.'

It is clear that the Lover is joined to Christ alone, and will not follow any monastic name, founder, or rule. It is his turn to ask questions, so he turns to the monks. 'Why do you who are *Religious* not take the Name of my Beloved? May it not be that, as you bear the name of another, your love may grow less, and that, hearing the voice of another, you may not catch the voice of my Beloved?'

Ramon Lull is a real Franciscan in this. The name, rule, or Order of Francis will never supplant the love of his Beloved Jesus, and it is the love and spirit of Jesus that makes Francis the universal brother of all.

There is no Franciscan spirituality apart from the gospel, no name, no rule, no teaching, and no way but the spirit and life of Jesus. Indeed, it is Francis who enables us to see more clearly the universality of Jesus when so many parts of the Church, and so many sects, domesticate and tame Jesus to their own liking, and manipulate the gospel to suit their own perspectives and standards.

In that sense, Francis has enabled me to see Jesus more clearly, and Francis has both filled me with a more profound love for Jesus, and scared me in the realization of what Jesus asks of me.

I see Jesus more clearly, hear Jesus more distinctly, feel Jesus more immediately, love Jesus more intimately. So now I ask myself the question: 'Do I follow Jesus now more closely?'

As we have been exploring Franciscan spirituality as an overflow of the gospel, there are three things that emerge:

First, Francis was identified with Jesus so closely that he was wounded with the sorrow and joy of Christ, which led him into the mystery of God.

Second, he allowed that mystery to radiate through his being, so that he became a brother to all humanity, to all living creatures, and to all creation.

Third, he allowed that mystery of love to become incarnate. He gave himself body, soul, and spirit for the alleviation of suffering and the redemption of all, through the love of Christ.

All the factual and embroidered stories of Francis reflect this Calvary love, and I encourage the reader of these words to follow and love Jesus Christ in the steps of the Poor Man of Assisi, who said, as he lay dying:

> 'I have done what was mine to do;
> may Christ teach you what is yours.'

References

INTRODUCTION: A DISTINCTIVE FRANCISCAN FLAVOUR

1 See the collection of essays from *The Way*, in Lavinia Byrne (ed.), *Traditions of Spiritual Guidance* (London: The Way Publications, 1992).

1 LOOKING FOR FRANCIS OF ASSISI

1 Nikos Kazantzakis, *St Francis* (Oxford: Bruno Cassiver, 1962), p. 22.
2 *The Daily Office SSF* (London: Mowbray, 1992), p. 283.

2 GALILEE, UMBRIA, AND WHERE I AM

1 E. Renan, quoted in Omer Englebert, *Saint Francis of Assisi* (London: Burns Oats, 1950), p. 13.
2 ibid., p. 19.
3 *1 Cel* 115 (*Omn* 329).
4 1 Corinthians 11.1.
5 A perusal of the writings of Leonardo Boff reveals how threatening such an application can be to a materialistic Church and culture. See especially *Saint Francis: A Model for Human Liberation* (New York: Crossroad, 1982).
6 Quoted in *Omn* 6.
7 *Sp* 93 (*Omn* 1226).

3 TROUBADOUR ROMANTICISM

1 Father Cuthbert OSFC, *Life of St Francis of Assisi* (London: Longmans Green, 1914), pp. 1–16.
2 Chretien de Troyes, quoted in Julien Green, *God's Fool* (London: Hodder and Stoughton, 1986), p. 41.
3 *1 Cel* 7 (*Omn* 235).
4 Omer Englebert, *Saint Francis of Assisi* (1950), pp. 43–4.
5 *Legenda antiqua*.
6 This story is beautifully told in the *Fioretti* (*Omn* 1429ff.).
7 G. K. Chesterton writes lyrically of Francis as a man in love, confounding the worldly wise, in *St Francis of Assisi* (London: Hodder and Stoughton, 1923), pp. 14–17.

8 *Sp* 93 (*Omn* 1226f.).

9 ibid., 96 (*Omn* 1230).

10 Quoted in Vida D. Scudder, *The Franciscan Adventure* (London: J. M. Dent, 1931), p. 335.

11 Brother Ramon SSF, *Jacopone* (London: HarperCollins, 1990), pp. 212ff.

12 Father Cuthbert OSFC, *Life of St Francis of Assisi* (1914), pp. 13f.

4 SUFFERING AND DISILLUSION

1 Quoted in Elizabeth Goudge, *Saint Francis of Assisi* (London: Hodder and Stoughton, 1959), pp. 22f.

2 *2 Cel* 4 (*Omn* 364).

3 Paul Sabatier, *Life of St Francis of Assisi* (London: Hodder and Stoughton, 1894), p. 16.

4 *2 Cel* 6 (*Omn* 366).

5 ibid.

6 Margaret of Cortona's story is well told in Cecily Hallack and Peter F. Anson, *These Made Peace* (London: Burns Oats, 1957), pp. 74–82.

7 See Brother Ramon SSF, *A Hidden Fire* (Basingstoke: Marshall Pickering, 1985), pp. 177ff. Ewart Cousins, in his Introduction to Bonaventure's *The Life of St Francis*, traces the inner order of chapter V–XIII according to the three stages of *purgation*, *illumination*, and *perfection (union)*. (London: SPCK, 1978), pp. 43f.

5 EVANGELICAL CONVERSION

1 Esther de Waal, *Seeking God: The Way of St Benedict* (London: Collins Fount, 1984), p. 70.

2 Matthew 11.28–30.

3 Angela of Foligno, *The Book of Divine Consolation*, Treatise I.

4 Bonaventure, *The Soul's Journey to God*, Prologue 4.

5 Exodus 3.1–12.

6 Jeremiah 1.5.

7 Isaiah 6.8.

8 Galatians 1.15–16.

9 John Moorman, *A History of the Franciscan Order* (Oxford: OUP, 1968) pp. 5f., and *St Francis of Assisi*, pp. 4ff.

10 *3S* 7 (*Omn* 896).

11 Julien Green, *God's Fool* (1986), p. 71.

12 *3S* 14 (*Omn* 904).

13 This section is based primarily on E. Allison Peers, *Ramon Lull* (London: SPCK, 1929), and *Fool of Love* (London: SPCK, 1946).

6 SERVING AND BUILDING

1 *3S* 11 (*Omn* 900).
2 *Testament* (*Omn* 67).
3 *LM* 5–6 (*Omn* 638ff.); *Lm* 8 (*Omn* 797f.).
4 *LM* 4 (*Omn* 643).
5 Duane Arnold and George Fry, *Francis — A Call to Conversion* (London: SPCK, 1988), pp. 26f.
6 *3S* 21 (*Omn* 911).
7 *1 Cel* 18 (*Omn* 244).
8 *3S* 24 (*Omn* 913f.).
9 *Fior* 30 (*Omn* 1376).
10 ibid., 5 (*Omn* 1313f.).
11 Ephesians 2.21f.; 1 Peter 1.5.

7 COMMUNITY OF LOVE

1 *Testament* (*Omn* 68).
2 *Book of the Lover and the Beloved*, 50, 68.
3 *3S* 23 (*Omn* 913).
4 Murray Bodo, *The Way of St Francis* (London: Collins Fount, 1984), p. 65.
5 *3S* 23 (*Omn* 913).
6 Bodo, *The Way of St Francis* (1984), pp. 68ff.
7 Brother Ramon SSF, *Forty Days and Forty Nights* (London: HarperCollins, 1993), pp. 232ff.
8 Matthew 10.7–13.
9 *1 Cel* 23 (*Omn* 247f.).
10 Matthew 19.21; Luke 9.3; Matthew 16.24; see *3S* 29 (*Omn* 918).
11 *LP* 114 (*Omn* 1088f.).
12 Duane Arnold and George Fry, *Francis — A Call to Conversion* (1988), p. 50.
13 *1 Cel* 23 (*Omn* 248).
14 *1 Cel* 27 (*Omn* 250f.).

8 THE EVANGELICAL COUNSELS

1 Omer Englebert, *Saint Francis of Assisi* (London: Burns Oats, 1950), p. 38.

2 *Fior* 2 (*Omn* 1305).

3 *Omn* 118f.

4 Robert Van de Weyer, *The Way of Holiness* (London: HarperCollins, 1992), p. 91.

5 Brother Ramon SSF, *Jacopone* (1990), pp. 111f.

6 Brother Ramon SSF, *Forty Days and Forty Nights* (1993), p. 38.

7 *2 Cel* 152 (*Omn* 484f.).

8 *Omn* 1839.

9 ibid., 1837.

10 *3S* 33 (*Omn* 921).

11 ibid., 34 (*Omn* 922).

9 BROTHERS AND SISTERS

1 G. K. Chesterton parallels the significance of an earthly and a heavenly love: *St Francis of Assisi* (1923), pp. 126–9.

2 Julien Green, *God's Fool* (1986), pp. 143ff.

3 Anthony Mockler, *Francis of Assisi: The Wandering Years* (Oxford: Phaidon, 1976), pp. 169, 171.

4 Clifton Wolters (ed.), *The Letters of Abelard and Heloise* (Harmondsworth: Penguin Books, 1974), pp. 132ff.

5 Green, *God's Fool*, p. 146.

6 Murray Bodo, *The Way of St Francis* (1984), pp. 50f.

7 *Omn* 72.

8 Quoted in Eric Doyle, *St Francis and the Song of Brotherhood* (London: Allen and Unwin, 1980), p. 22.

9 Quoted in Lord Longford, *Francis of Assisi* pp. 48f.

10 ibid., pp. 50f.

11 ibid., p. 52.

12 Quoted in Sister Francis Teresa OSC, *Living the Incarnation* (London: Darton, Longman and Todd, 1993), p. 92.

13 ibid.

14 John Moorman, *A History of the Franciscan Order* (1968), pp. 260f.

15 Quoted in Longford, *Francis of Assisi*, pp. 53f.

16 Sister Francis Teresa, *Living the Incarnation* (1993), p. 93.

10 MISSIONARY FERVOUR

1 See Vida D. Scudder, *The Franciscan Adventure* (1931), p. 47; Omer Englebert, *Saint Francis of Assisi* (1950), pp. 178f.

2 Romans 10.2; Philippians 3.6.

3 *Sp* 65 (*Omn* 1191f.).

4 Quoted by Englebert, *Saint Francis of Assisi* (1950), p. 193.

5 *Chronicle of Jordan di Giano*, 5–6.

6 ibid., 18–19; see Englebert, *Saint Francis of Assisi* (1950), pp. 197f.

7 *The Rule of 1221*, 16 (*Omn* 43f.).

8 See John Moorman, 'Early Franciscan Missions', *A History of the Franciscan Order* (1968), pp. 226–39.

9 E. Allison Peers, *Fool of Love* (1946).

10 Quoted in Moorman, *A History of the Franciscan Order* (1968), p. 257.

11 ibid., pp. 238f.

12 *2 Cel* 30 (*Omn* 388f.).

13 *LM* 8 (*Omn* 704).

11 THE THIRD ORDER

1 *1 Cel* 36 (*Omn* 259).

2 *Fior* 16 (*Omn* 1335f.).

3 *1 Cel* 37 (*Omn* 259f.).

4 See Father Cuthbert OSFC, *Life of St Francis of Assisi* (1914), pp. 325f.

5 *Omn* 93.

6 2 Samuel 23.8ff.; Luke 10.1.

7 Cuthbert, *Life of St Francis of Assisi* (1914), p. 332.

8 See ibid., pp. 332f.

9 *Significatum nobis*; see Cuthbert, *Life of St Francis of Assisi* (1914), p. 341.

10 See ibid., p. 341.

11 Quoted in Omer Englebert, *Saint Francis of Assisi* (1950), p. 238.

12 Excellent chapters on the Third Order appear in John Moorman, *A History of the Franciscan Order* (1968), pp. 40ff.; 216ff.; 417ff.; 560ff.

13 See *The Daily Office SSF* (London: Mowbray, 1992), pp. 301ff.

14 Cuthbert, *Life of St Francis of Assisi*, p. 345; see also Englebert, *Saint Francis of Assisi*, pp. 239f., and Elizabeth Goudge, *Saint Francis of Assisi*, p. 153.

12 FRANCISCAN PRAYING

1 See Roger D. Sorrell, *St Francis of Assisi and Nature* (New York: OUP, 1988), pp. 7f.

2 See *Fior, LP, Sp, 3S*.

3 *LM* VIII, 11 (*Omn* 697f.); see also *LM* XIII, 6–11 (*Omn* 692ff.); 2 *Cel* 165–71 (*Omn* 494ff.).
4 *LM* IX, 1 (*Omn* 698); also 2 *Cel* 165 (*Omn* 494f.).
5 *1 Cel* 80 (*Omn* 296).
6 *2 Cel* 9 (*Omn* 369).
7 See *3S* 28–9 (*Omn* 917f.); *Fior Consideration* 3 (*Omn* 1447f.).
8 John Moorman, *A History of the Franciscan Order*, p. 257.
9 *Opera Omnia* (Quaracchi), vol. VIII, p. 120.
10 *2 Cel* 94–5 (*Omn* 439ff.).
11 *2 Cel* 96 (*Omn* 441f.).
12 *The Daily Office SSF* (1992), p. 678.
13 *LM* IX, 2 (*Omn* 699).
14 *1 Cel* 96 (*Omn* 310f.).
15 *Fior* 11 (*Omn* 1323ff.).
16 *LM* III, 9–10 (*Omn* 652f.).
17 ibid., IX, 1–2 (*Omn* 288).
18 *1 Cel* 71 (*Omn* 288).
19 *3S* 14 (*Omn* 904).
20 *Fior* 2 (*Omn* 1302ff.).
21 Luke 18.38; Isaiah 6.3; Revelation 4.8.
22 Quoted in Cheslyn Jones *et al.* (eds), *The Study of Spirituality* (London: SPCK, 1986), p. 306.
23 *LM* X, 2 (*Omn* 706f.).
24 ibid., X, 2 (*Omn* 706).
25 See ibid., X, 3–5 (*Omn* 707ff.).
26 Meditation 6.

13 ECOLOGY AND RECONCILIATION

1 See Esther de Waal, *The Celtic Vision* (London: Darton, Longman and Todd, 1988), and *A World Made Whole: Rediscovering the Celtic Tradition* (London: HarperCollins, 1991).
2 Sean McDonagh, *To Care for the Earth* (London: Chapman, 1986), p. 130.
3 ibid., pp. 133f.
4 *Omn* 296ff.
5 Wendell Berry, *The Gift of Good Land*, p. 113, quoted in McDonagh, *To Care for the Earth*, p. 76.
6 *LM* VIII, 1 (*Omn* 688).

14 THE CANTICLE OF BROTHER SUN

1 Text from Omer Englebert, *Saint Francis of Assisi* (Chicago: Franciscan Herald Press, 1965), p. 458.
2 Translation by Placid Hermann, *Omn* 130f.
3 *LP* 43 (*Omn* 1020).
4 ibid.; cf. *2 Cel* 213 (*Omn* 532f.).
5 2 Corinthians 4.6f.
6 Eloi Leclerc OFM, *The Canticle of Creatures: Symbols of Union* (Chicago: Franciscan Herald Press, 1970), p. xi.
7 *1 Cel* 47 (*Omn* 268f.).
8 Leclerc, *The Canticle of Creatures* (1970), p. xiii.
9 Thomas of Spalato describes Francis' spirit-anointed preaching at Bologna in 1222, which reconciled secular feuds (*Omn* 1601f.). At a Chapter, Francis made it clear that peace in the world can only be secured if there is peace in the heart. See *3S* 58 (*Omn* 942f.).
10 *1 Cel* 23 (*Omn* 248); also *Testament* (*Omn* 68).
11 *LP* 44 (*Omn* 1024); see also *Sp* 101 (*Omn* 1237ff.).
12 The story of my objection and tribunal is told in Brother Ramon SSF, *Fulness of Joy* (Basingstoke: Marshall Pickering, 1988), pp. 95–102. Lord Longford, in *Francis of Assisi*, has a fair and moving chapter on 'St Francis and Peace', in which he wrestles with the problems of being a Christian and Franciscan in a violent world.
13 Leclerc, *The Canticle of Creatures* (1970), pp. 227ff.

15 SISTER BODILY DEATH

1 *Sp* 121 (*Omn* 1261f.).
2 ibid., 122 (*Omn* 1262f.).
3 ibid., 123 (*Omn* 1264).
4 *de Exhort. Mart.* 13 quoted in H. B. Workman, *Persecution in the Early Church* (Oxford: OUP), p. 327.
5 Eloi Leclerc OFM, *The Canticle of Creatures: Symbols of Union* (1970), p. 181.
6 *Omn* 98.
7 Dylan Thomas, *Selected Works* (London: J. M. Dent, 1976), p. 79.
8 Ellen Goodman, *The Guardian Weekly*, 7 February 1993.
9 Maurice Rawlings, *Beyond Death's Door* (London: Sheldon, 1978), p. 124.
10 Elisabeth Kübler-Ross, *On Death and Dying* (London: Tavistock Publications, 1970).

11 Cicely Saunders, *Beyond All Pain* (London: SPCK), esp. pp. 61ff.
12 Kübler-Ross, *On Death and Dying*; Raymond Moody, *Life After Life* (Illinois: Bantam Books, 1986); *Reflections on Life After Life* (New York: Avon Book); Karlis Osis and Erlendur Haraldsson, *At the Hour of Death*.
13 Moody, *Life After Life* (1986), pp. 5f.
14 *1 Cel* 48 (*Omn* 269f.).
15 *Sp* 124 (*Omn* 1265).

16 MYSTICAL LIFE

1 F. C. Happold, *Mysticism* (Harmondsworth: Penguin, 1963), p. 19.
2 Psalm 104.29f.
3 Not the Dionysius of Acts 17.34; see 'Denys the Areopagite', in Gordon S. Wakefield (ed.), *A Dictionary of Christian Spirituality* (London: SCM, 1983), pp. 108f.
4 See Ewart Cousins, *Bonaventure* (1978), pp. 43f.
5 *2 Cel* 9 (*Omn* 369f.).
6 ibid., 156 (*Omn* 487f.); 161f. (*Omn* 491f.); *LM* 6 (*Omn* 666f.).
7 Galatians 6.7.
8 *Omn* 110.
9 St John of the Cross (*Spiritual Canticle*, IX, V, 6–7) says that there is weariness of heart at this stage as long as the believer does not truly possess that which it loves. Such a one is like a hungry person longing for food, an invalid sighing for health, or one who is suspended in the air with no firm foothold.
10 *Fior* 25 (*Omn* 1358).
11 John Eudes Bamberger, *Continuum* 7.2 (1968), p. 238.
12 *The Daily Office SSF* (1992), p. 294.

17 STIGMATA: UNION IN LOVE

1 *Fior Consideration 3* (*Omn* 1448).
2 Galatians 2.19–20; Philippians 3.10; Colossians 1.24.
3 Omer Englebert, *Saint Francis of Assisi* (1950), p. 281, from *LM* XIII, 3 (*Omn* 730f.).
4 *LM* XIII, 4 (*Omn* 731).
5 Cf. *2 Cel* 135–8 (*Omn* 472–4); *1 Cel* 95 (*Omn* 309f.).
6 *LM* XIII, 8 (*Omn* 734).
7 See Genesis 28.10–22; 32.22–31.
8 See Galatians 6.14–17.

9 *New English Hymnal* (Norwich: The Canterbury Press, 1986), no. 350.

10 *Fior* 2 (*Omn* 1302f.).

11 D. N. S. Nicholson (ed.), *The Oxford Book of English Mystical Verse* (Oxford: OUP, 1917), pp. 512ff.

12 *L'Osservatore Romano*, 16 June 1971, quoted in *FB* 155f.

13 Quoted in *FB* 101.

18 FRANCIS AND FRANCISCANS

1 See Paul Sabatier, 'The Crisis of the Order', *Life of St Francis of Assisi* (1894), pp. 239ff.

2 Sermon II in Bonaventure's collection, quoted in Eric Doyle, *St Francis and the Song of Brotherhood* (1980), p. 180.

3 See Anne Macdonell, *Sons of Francis* (London: J. M. Dent, 1902), pp. 60, 63f.

4 See Brother Ramon SSF, *Jacopone* (1990), chs 7 and 8 (pp. 78ff. and 88ff.).

5 *Omn* 71ff.

6 ibid.; *1 Cel* 35 (*Omn* 257f.).

7 See Cecily Hallack and Peter F. Anson, 'Hermits and Solitaries', *These Made Peace* (1957), pp. 107ff.

8 ibid., p. 117.

9 Published by SSF.

Index